Vicki Howie is a popular and well

wide range of resources includes *Easy Ways to Seas...*
Ways to Bible Fun for the Very Young, *Easy Ways to Seasonal Fun for the Very Young* and the highly successful *Easy Ways to Christmas Plays*, Volumes 1 and 2. She has also contributed to Barnabas' full-colour range with titles such as *On Easter Day in the Morning* and *Silent Night*, and has written for the 7–11s with her popular title, *Story Plays for Christmas*.

Barnabas
for
Children®

Barnabas for Children® is a registered word mark and the logo is a registered device mark of The Bible Reading Fellowship.

Text copyright © Vicki Howie 2012
Illustrations copyright © Paula Doherty 2012
The author asserts the moral right
to be identified as the author of this work

Published by
The Bible Reading Fellowship
15 The Chambers, Vineyard
Abingdon OX14 3FE
United Kingdom
Tel: +44 (0)1865 319700
Email: enquiries@brf.org.uk
Website: www.brf.org.uk
BRF is a Registered Charity

ISBN 978 1 84101 853 9

First published 2012
10 9 8 7 6 5 4 3 2 1 0

Acknowledgments
Unless otherwise stated, scripture quotations are taken from the Contemporary English Version of the Bible published by HarperCollins Publishers, copyright © 1991, 1992, 1995 American Bible Society.

The paper used in the production of this publication was supplied by mills that source their raw materials from sustainably managed forests. Soy-based inks were used in its printing and the laminate film is biodegradable.

A catalogue record for this book is available from the British Library

Printed in Singapore by Craft Print International Ltd

Seasonal Activities

for

Christmas Festivities

Three five-week programmes exploring the true
meaning of Christmas with 7–11s

Vicki Howie

✷ *For my husband Douglas* ✷

Acknowledgments

With thanks to my nieces, Kasia and Sabine, then aged 9 and 11, who thought up many of the 'Suggestions might include…' answers to the questions posed by the leader.

Thank you to Revd Richard Worssam and Christeen Malan, Sunday club leader with 7–11s, for their help and advice.

Thanks also to Lucy Moore for the inspiration behind the ideas in the fifth session of the first programme ('Jesus') about what we do with a present.

★

Contents

Foreword

How I wish I'd had this marvellous resource from Vicki Howie when I was a parish-based children and youth minister! It would have saved me many hours of searching and wondering how to present the Christmas story 'slightly differently' to save the children (and myself) from becoming over-familiar with and inattentive to the beauty and wonder of the greatest event in history.

With potentially three years' worth of material in this one volume, the three five-week programmes are creative in their approach to unwrapping, unpacking and exploring the gift of Christmas in ways that children and their leaders alike will find creative and engaging.

And there lies the greatest thing about this book. The best resources for nurturing children in faith are the ones that encourage, challenge and nurture adults in their faith too. As Vicki says, 'It is a wonderful thing that the Christian faith encourages us to ask questions and seek out the truth (Matthew 7:7–9)'. Sometimes adults forget the wonder of asking questions and become more concerned that they don't know the answer. Often the value is in the asking. Throughout each of these programmes Vicki gently demonstrates how to open up questions and wondering alongside games, drama, craft activities, prayer and discussion, that the adult with an open heart and mind will find as enriching as the children.

I have great pleasure in heartily commending this resource to you, with its nuggets and gems of wisdom. Here's just one to close with: 'It could be Christmas every day if we did the little loving things for other people that we know please God instead of striving for "the perfect Christmas" just once a year' (p. 54).

Yvonne Morris
Diocesan Children's Adviser for the Diocese of Oxford

★

Introduction

This book contains three five-week programmes exploring three separate but interlinked Christmas themes. The material fits readily into the autumn half-term leading up to Christmas, and a short Christmas presentation, summarising what the children have discovered, is included with each programme for possible inclusion in a Christmas service.

The programmes and their themes are as follows.

1. **Christmas unwrapped:** The first programme unwraps the five layers of a Christmas present to discover a different nativity figure each week. We explore what each character gave as a gift at the first Christmas and think about how we might reflect that gift today. For example, Mary gave her willingness, and we think how we might develop a willing attitude.

2. **Christmas unpacked:** The second programme unpacks a Christmas stocking week by week to find five small gifts. These gifts lead to five Bible stories, beginning with Adam and Eve and ending with the Easter story, which chart God's ongoing compassion and put Christmas in context. We discover that Christmas is a very important festival because we are celebrating the birth of the one who came to mend our broken relationship with God.

3. **The gift of Christmas:** The final programme leads us from five Christmas Bible stories to discover people Jesus came to befriend. Each week, a tree decoration is made from a gift tag to symbolise a particular group of people. The decorations serve as a reminder of people we can remember at Christmas, such as those who are homeless or lonely, and those who have been forced to flee from their homes and countries.

Within each programme, the five sessions follow the same pattern and include the following sections.

Ready, steady...

Sets out the aim of the session and provides a short Bible reflection to aid the teaching of the material.

Go!

An introduction to the theme, designed to stimulate thinking.

Icebreaker

An activity to get the children talking, moving and thinking about the theme.

Dramatised Bible story

A Bible reading designed to be divided among several children, with two questions to puzzle out, to encourage careful listening.

Drama games

A choice of simple games, some lively and others more meditative, to explore the theme further, introduce humour and enjoyment and use up energy in a controlled way. Many of the suggestions are followed by a discussion to link the game to the theme and its relevance for today.

Follow-up discussion

Suggestions to tease out the theme and teaching of an activity.

Craft activities (group and individual)

A choice of simple crafts based on the theme.

Prayer

Suggestions for prayer to draw together the threads of the session and ask God for help in putting the ideas into action this Christmas and beyond.

Party bag

An activity providing something that the children can take away with them to try out at home.

Above all, *Seasonal Activities for Christmas Festivities* is designed for enjoyment. The ideas are offered to encourage the celebration of Christmas in a way that is satisfying and pleasing to God.

Christmas unwrapped

Themes

Being willing; being a true friend; being watchful; having a sense of wonder; giving the gift of love

Introduction

Christmas is a time for giving and receiving. 'Christmas unwrapped' has been written to help us think more about what we might give at Christmas rather than what we might receive. Each session looks closely at the nativity story, unwrapping it week by week, layer by layer, and focusing on the key nativity characters in order to discover what gift or personal quality he or she gave at the first Christmas.

As each gift is discovered and the theme is developed through a choice of lively games, Bible study, simple craft and thoughtful discussion, we are encouraged to think how we might reflect the same nativity gift over the coming Christmas season and beyond.

The theme is explored through a multi-wrapped Christmas present (rather like a pass-the-parcel present), which is unwrapped over the course of the sessions. The present needs to be wrapped in advance, incorporating figures from a nativity set between the five layers of wrapping. Start by wrapping the figure of baby Jesus, as he is the gift, followed by the wise men, some shepherds, Joseph and, finally, Mary, who will be the first character unwrapped.

Read through all the programme material beforehand, including the presentation on pages 65–70, which acts as a summary. Ideally, encourage any helpers to do the same so that everyone is working towards the same goal.

If you are going to perform the presentation, perhaps within a Christmas service, you might like to start making any practical arrangements for this well in advance.

Mary

Theme
Being willing

Bible story
Luke 1:26–56

Ready, steady...

The angel Gabriel visits Mary with the tremendous news that she is to be Jesus' mother. God often asks ordinary people to help him do extraordinary things. Sometimes we are reluctant, feeling inadequate for the task, but being willing to play our part is not so much to do with any particular skill as with the knowledge that God will be there to help us. For example, when Moses asked, 'Who am I to go to the king and lead your people out of Egypt?' God answered, 'I will be with you' (Exodus 3:11–12).

In contrast to Moses, young David faced Goliath with confidence, trusting that God would help him. His response to Goliath was, 'The Lord always wins his battles, and he will help us defeat you' (1 Samuel 17:47).

At the angel's greeting, Mary was confused. When she was told that she would be the mother of God's Son, she asked a practical question. On hearing the answer, her trust in God was such that she accepted her role humbly and willingly before praising God for the part she had been chosen to play in the Christmas story.

What makes us willing (or unwilling) to respond positively to someone's request for help? Sometimes we lack confidence in our own abilities or perhaps we find it hard to put ourselves in another's shoes. The activities in the session aim to help us to overcome these difficulties.

Go!

Display the multi-wrapped Christmas present in a prominent place and talk about the fact that it is nearly the season of Advent, when we look forward to Christmas. Chat together about what the children like about Christmas. Join in with their enthusiasm and hold up the present if anyone mentions receiving gifts.

Explain that Christmas is a time of giving because we are reflecting God's great gift to us—his Son, Jesus. Go on to say that, over the next few weeks, you'll be unwrapping the Christmas story, layer by layer, week by week, focusing on the different nativity characters to find out what each of them gave at the first Christmas. Their gifts may not have been things we can hold or touch, but perhaps a personal/quality, such as kindness or boldness. Encourage everyone to be Christmas detectives, on the lookout for these gifts.

Think together about what getting ready for Christmas involves. What extra tasks might people need to do? Suggestions might include shopping (for cards, presents and food); writing cards and adding news; preparing for visitors (cleaning and making up beds); decorating the house.

Icebreaker

You will need

Two containers, one marked 'Yes' and one marked 'No'; twelve postcards, each marked with one of the following replies and hidden around the room beforehand.

- Of course!
- I can!
- Straightaway!
- Certainly!
- I'd love to!
- Thanks for asking me!
- Of course not!
- I can't!
- Maybe later!
- Certainly not!
- I don't want to!
- No thanks!

Chat together about how we might answer when someone at home asks for help with a job. Do we say 'yes' (hold up the container marked 'yes') or 'no' (hold up the other container)? Explain that there are different ways of saying 'yes' and 'no'.

Divide the group into two teams. One team is 'yes' and the other is 'no'. Explain that there are twelve answers to a request for help hidden around the room. The 'yes' team should look for the six replies that mean 'yes' and post them in the appropriate box. The 'no' team do the same with the negative answers.

Alternatively, mix up the cards and place them face downwards on the floor. Ask different children to come and pick up a card, read it to the group and say whether they think it should be placed under the 'yes' or the 'no' heading.

Discuss the different answers. Do they sound enthusiastic and willing? Do they sound polite? Why might someone answer in this way? How might this make the person who asked for help feel? Would we feel comfortable answering like this?

When all the cards have been sorted, think together about what the word 'willing' means. On a scale of 1 to 10, how willing are we? Perhaps that depends upon what we are being asked to do! What makes us more willing to say 'yes'? Suggestions might include loving, liking or trusting the person asking for help; understanding that the person needs help; admiring or agreeing with what the person is trying to do; feeling pleased, proud or privileged to have been asked; knowing that the task is something we can do (even though we might need help); realising that doing it might help us as much as it helps the person asking (we might learn a lot from it); remembering that the person has helped us in the past, and so on.

Chat about times when we might be less willing to say 'yes'. This might be a good opportunity to emphasise that there are times when it is good to say 'no'—for example, when someone is putting us under pressure to do something wrong. End the icebreaker by matching the 'yes' responses with their opposite 'no' responses.

Dramatised Bible story

Explain that today's Christmas Bible story is about someone who needed to decide what to answer when God asked for her help. Choose someone to unwrap the first layer of the Christmas present, to reveal Mary.

Try to bring the character of Mary alive by discussing how old she was at the time of the Christmas story, what kind of house she lived in, what kind of things she might have done to help at home, and so on.

Background to the story

Mary was probably about 14 years old when the angel Gabriel visited her. She probably wore a tunic that went down to the ankles and was fastened with a belt at the waist. She would have worn her hair long, perhaps arranged in plaits. Mary would have lived in a simple house in the small town of Nazareth. Many houses only had one room with one small window (without glass), high up, and one door. The room would have been lit by a little oil lamp. There were usually two levels inside the house. The lower area, near the door, had a floor made of flattened earth. The family brought their animals, such as a donkey, some sheep and a guard dog, into this area at night. The upper level was where the family ate meals together, talked and slept. The house would have had a flat roof made of wooden branches laid across thick wooden beams.

Mary would have been expected to help her mother with the daily jobs. These would have included grinding grain into flour for bread, baking the bread, fetching water from a nearby spring or well, tidying and sweeping the house and washing clothes.

Before you read the story together, ask the children to listen carefully to discover what God's messenger asked Mary to do and how Mary replied. The story can be divided among several children.

Narrator 1:	God sent the angel Gabriel to the town of Nazareth in Galilee with a message for a virgin named Mary. She was engaged to Joseph from the family of King David. The angel greeted Mary and said…
Angel:	You are truly blessed! The Lord is with you.
Narrator 2:	Mary was confused by the angel's words and wondered what they meant. Then the angel told Mary…

Reproduced with permission from *Seasonal Activities for Christmas Festivities* by Vicki Howie (BRF/Barnabas, 2012)

www.barnabasinchurches.org.uk

Angel:	Don't be afraid! God is pleased with you, and you will have a son. His name will be Jesus. He will be great and will be called the Son of God Most High. The Lord God will make him king, as his ancestor David was. He will rule the people of Israel for ever, and his kingdom will never end.
Narrator 3:	Mary asked the angel…
Mary:	How can this happen? I am not married!
Narrator 3:	The angel answered…
Angel:	The Holy Spirit will come down to you, and God's power will come over you. So your child will be called the holy Son of God. Your relative Elizabeth is also going to have a son, even though she is old. No one thought she could ever have a baby, but in three months she will have a son. Nothing is impossible for God!
Narrator 4:	Mary said…
Mary:	I am the Lord's servant! Let it happen as you have said.
Narrator 1:	And the angel left her.
Narrator 2:	A short time later, Mary hurried to visit her relative Elizabeth. She greeted Elizabeth and then sang out…
Mary:	With all my heart I praise the Lord and I am glad because of God my Saviour. He cares for me, his humble servant. From now on, all people will say that God has blessed me. God All-Powerful has done great things for me, and his name is holy.

Reproduced with permission from *Seasonal Activities for Christmas Festivities* by Vicki Howie (BRF/Barnabas, 2012)
www.barnabasinchurches.org.uk

Follow-up discussion

Chat about how the angel Gabriel asked Mary to be Jesus' mother. Although she was surprised at first and had a question to ask, Mary loved and trusted God and quickly replied with a joyful 'Yes!' Mary's Christmas gift was her willingness.

Drama games

Tasks

The aim of this game is to help everyone to get to know each other better and to stimulate imagination. Acting in a willing manner is halfway to being willing.

Everyone stands and finds a partner. Give them a couple of minutes to chat about tasks that they like and don't like at home or at school.

Now everyone stands in a circle. One person starts the game by asking the person on their left for help with a task that they like doing. For example, 'Will you help me decorate the Christmas tree?' The second person replies, 'Yes! I'd love to!' This person then asks the person on their left for help with a different task, and so on all round the circle.

Repeat the game in the opposite direction with less popular tasks. Encourage everyone to use their imagination to make the tasks sound truly uninviting. For example, 'Will you help me do loads of washing up?' However, explain that the reply, 'Yes! I'd love to!' must sound genuine and enthusiastic. They will really have to act. If anyone speaks through gritted teeth, ask them to try again.

Follow-up discussion

Chat together about how we could be more willing to do things we don't enjoy doing. For example, does it help to say 'yes' with enthusiasm, even though we may not feel enthusiastic? Could this be a first step?

Obstacle course

You will need

Some simple objects to make an obstacle course (see below); a blindfold

The aim of this game is to help anyone who feels they lack the confidence to undertake a task. Ask the children to help you build a simple obstacle course with everyday objects, such as a shoebox to step over, some plastic cups to weave around, a chair to circle and a draped rug or coat to crawl underneath. Make start and finishing points.

Ask for a confident volunteer to negotiate the course without touching any of the objects. As he or she prepares to start, explain that you forgot to mention that you would like them to wear a blindfold! Will this make a difference? Allow the volunteer to choose a friend to lead them and talk them over, around and under the obstacles. If there is time, let others have a go.

Follow-up discussion

Finish by chatting together about what sort of thing we don't like to be asked to do because it seems a bit scary. Be ready with an example of your own, and don't press anyone to answer. Explain that our lives can sometimes be like an obstacle course because we are faced with things that seem difficult. However, although we cannot see him, God is at our side, helping and guiding us (perhaps through the friends he provides for us). God loves us and wants the best for us, and he will never ask us to do anything that we cannot manage with his help.

Group craft

You will need

Thin card or paper; scissors; pencils; crayons; a long length of ribbon; a stapler

Ask everyone to draw a pair of mitten shapes on card by drawing around their hands. They should keep the wrist on the bottom edge of the card, the fingers together and the thumb slightly apart. Cut out the two shapes and explain that they represent willing hands.

As you make the willing hands, start to bring together all the things that you have been talking about in this session. What did God ask Mary to help him to do? What answer did she give to the angel? Was she willing or unwilling? How can we be more willing to do things for God?

Point out that God loves to do his work through our willing hands. Ask the children to think of one thing that they might be willing to do at home or at school to help someone else over Christmas. Ask them to write their idea or draw a picture of it on one of the hands. Staple the decorated hand shapes (from the straight wrist ends) at intervals along the ribbon, rather like a string of flags. Use this to decorate your meeting place.

Individual craft

You will need

Circles of white card (one per child); pencils; crayons; short lengths of ribbon (one per child); a hole punch

Make 'joyful Mary' gift tags. The children draw and colour Mary's smiling face on one side of the card circle. Punch a hole in the top and thread the ribbon through so that it can be attached to a present.

Ask the children to write 'Happy Christmas' on the back, and remind them that Mary felt happy and blessed to be Jesus' mother. Just an ordinary girl, she trusted God to help her play this important part.

If you are planning to perform the presentation on pages 65–70, you might like to keep some gift tags for the performance.

Prayer

If the children made 'willing hands', invite them to put the spare hand shape between their hands as they settle down to pray.

Dear God, please help us to remember that Christmas is much more about the things we can give than the things we might receive. Thank you for Mary, who gave the answer 'yes' to God. Please help us to reflect Mary's gift of willingness by having a willing attitude and by being your cheerful helpers, especially over the coming Christmas season. Amen

Party bag

Give the children a hand shape to take home as a reminder to have a willing attitude. They could write on it anything they manage to do willingly over the next week. Point out that the hand shape could also be seen as God's hand, giving us the opportunity to help others or learn new skills.

★

Joseph

Theme
Being a true friend

Bible story
Matthew 1:18–25; 2:13–23; Luke 2:1–7

Ready, steady...

God often provides someone in a prominent role with the help and support of a relative or friend. In the last session, we saw that Moses did not, at first, feel up to the job of leading the Israelites out of slavery in Egypt. He felt inadequate for the task, especially as he was not a good public speaker. But God promised to help him and provided him with the support of his brother, Aaron, who did the talking for him at a meeting of all the Israelites and before the king of Egypt (Exodus 4:27—5:1). It is interesting to see how Moses grew into the role, however, once Aaron had led the way.

After David—a simple shepherd boy—defeated Goliath, he enjoyed the close friendship and support of Jonathan, King Saul's son. The two made a promise to be friends for life (1 Samuel 18—19). Jonathan had the courage to speak up for David in front of his father, who was jealous of David's success and popularity, and later protected David by warning him of Saul's plan to kill him.

The New Testament refers to Joanna, Susanna and other women who travelled with Jesus and the twelve disciples, helping to support them out of their own means (Luke 8:1–3). In Acts 13—14, we read that Barnabas travelled with Paul, encouraging him and helping him to set up new churches. Together, they faced threats and beatings from local people.

Read Matthew 1:18–25; Luke 2:1–7 and Matthew 2:13–23, noting all the ways in which Joseph supported Mary and protected his new family. His actions (some of which are implied by the biblical text) are listed on page 29.

The Bible does not record anything spoken by Joseph. However, his actions say a lot about him. He must have been a kind and compassionate man, for we are told that he planned to divorce Mary quietly (an engagement was legally binding at that time) in order to avoid embarrassing her in public. He was a man of great faith, for he obeyed God at once and without question. He was also a principled man, concerned to do what was right, even at the cost of his own reputation. He took Mary into his home as his wife, although others must have doubted Mary's story about the baby.

Think about a true friend. What makes that person so special? How do true friends support us? Perhaps they drop everything to come to our aid in a crisis. Perhaps they accompany us on difficult days and give us moral support. True friends believe in us and our projects or ambitions, even when others doubt.

Friends are very important to us all and we need to work hard at maintaining our friendships. Social networking sites help us to keep in touch, but there is a difference between internet 'friends', of which we may have hundreds, and true friends. There is a danger that we may sit alone at the computer rather than mixing with the people around us.

How can we, as adults, be true friends to the children we know? Whenever the opportunity arises, we should show genuine interest in their hobbies, plans and concerns. We can also encourage them to support each other as they continue on their Christian journeys together. Such friendship will be of great value to them as they enter their teenage years, when they may face questioning about their faith from peers, and school becomes more demanding.

Go!

Display the Christmas present, now with four layers of wrapping remaining. Talk about a particularly special Christmas present that you or a member of your family may have received, which came with instructions for its care. Examples might be the washing instructions for a jumper or the cleaning instructions for a pair of boots. Ask what might happen if the instructions were not followed. Stress the importance of looking after things.

Icebreaker

You will need

Five postcards, each marked with one of the following words: a pot plant; a silver bracelet; a pet; your hair; a friendship

Place the first four cards face downwards on the floor so that the words are hidden, but keep back the card marked 'a friendship'. Invite someone to pick up a card and to read it to the group. Encourage everyone to suggest some care instructions for the thing written on the card. How many can they think up for each card? In each case, ask what might happen if these instructions were not followed.

Now do the same with the card marked 'a friendship'. Do we need to look after our friendships? How can we do this? Ideas might include sharing in a friend's excitement, disappointment, happiness or sadness (this involves listening to them and trying to understand how they feel); encouraging a friend in all that they are trying to do and praising their work; thinking the best of our friends, speaking up for them and not passing on gossip about them; keeping in touch, especially if our friend moves away (Christmas is a good time to do this); showing a friend how to do something they are finding difficult at school, and leading the way; including a new friend in our games with others.

What can happen if we do not work hard at being a true friend?

Dramatised Bible story

Recap the part Mary played in the Christmas story and how she gave the gift of her willingness. Explain that today's Bible story is all about someone who looked after, or was a true friend to, Mary. Choose someone to unwrap the next layer of the Christmas present to reveal Joseph. Once again, try to bring the character of Joseph alive by exploring together what we know about him.

Background to the story

We do not know how old Joseph was at the time of the nativity, but it seems likely that he was a lot older than Mary. In those days, young people did not normally choose whom they would marry. Their parents chose for them. Once a wife had been chosen for a son, there were money arrangements to be made. The bride's parents had to be paid a sum for losing their daughter. However, the bride's father gave his daughter a special gift of money, called a dowry. Once all this was settled, the young couple became 'betrothed' or engaged to be married. The engagement lasted for a year, while all the preparations were being made for the wedding. It was legally binding and could only be broken by divorce.

Joseph was a carpenter and his work would have involved building houses and making furniture. He would have been a strong man, for carpenters had to cut down trees and shape the logs to use as beams for the roofs of houses. Joseph would also have made doors, tables, stools and chests for the home, as well as ploughs, yokes and shovels for farmers.

Before you read the story together, ask the children to listen carefully to see how many things they can discover that Joseph did to care for Mary and Jesus. The storytelling can be divided among several children.

Narrator 1:	This is how Jesus Christ was born. A young woman named Mary was engaged to be married to Joseph from King David's family. But before they were married, she learned that she was going to have a baby by God's Holy Spirit.
Narrator 2:	Joseph was a good man and did not want to embarrass Mary in front of everyone, so he decided to quietly call off the wedding.
Narrator 3:	While Joseph was thinking about this, an angel from the Lord came to him in a dream. The angel said…
Angel:	Joseph, the baby that Mary will have is from the Holy Spirit. Go ahead and marry her. Then, after her baby is born, name him Jesus, because he will save his people from their sins.
Narrator 4:	After Joseph woke up, he and Mary were soon married, just as the Lord's angel had told him to do.
Narrator 5:	Some months later, the Emperor Augustus gave orders for the names of all the people to be listed in record books. Everyone had to go to their own home town to be listed.
Narrator 6:	So Joseph had to leave Nazareth in Galilee and go to Bethlehem in Judea. Long ago, Bethlehem had been King David's home town, and Joseph went there because he was from David's family.

Reproduced with permission from *Seasonal Activities for Christmas Festivities* by Vicki Howie (BRF/Barnabas, 2012)
www.barnabasinchurches.org.uk

Narrator 1: Mary travelled with him. She was soon going to have a baby, and while they were there she gave birth to her firstborn son.

Narrator 2: She dressed him in baby clothes and laid him in a manger of hay, because there was no room for them in the inn.

Narrator 3: Some time later, an angel of the Lord appeared to Joseph in a dream and said...

Angel: Get up! Hurry and take the child and his mother to Egypt. Stay there until I tell you to return, because King Herod is looking for the child and wants to kill him.

Narrator 3: That night, Joseph got up and took his wife and the child to Egypt, where they stayed until Herod died.

Narrator 4: After King Herod died, an angel from the Lord appeared in a dream to Joseph while he was still in Egypt. The angel said...

Angel: Get up and take the child and his mother back to Israel. The people who wanted to kill him are now dead.

Narrator 5: Joseph got up and left with his family for Israel. But when he heard that Herod's son was now ruler of Judea, he was afraid to go there.

Narrator 6: Then, in a dream, he was told to go to Galilee, and they went to live there in the town of Nazareth.

Follow-up discussion

Chat together about the ways in which Joseph cared for Mary and Jesus. For example, he cared about Mary's feelings and did not

Reproduced with permission from *Seasonal Activities for Christmas Festivities* by Vicki Howie (BRF/Barnabas, 2012)
www.barnabasinchurches.org.uk

want to embarrass her. Before he was told by the angel that Mary's baby would be the Son of God, Joseph was planning to call off the wedding 'quietly'. Joseph married Mary and looked after her while she was expecting Jesus. He looked after her on the long journey to Bethlehem (about 70 miles). He may have led a little donkey on which Mary rode, and he probably made them a shelter to camp under each night and a fire on which to cook. He must have found someone kind in Bethlehem to give them shelter in a cave or stable. He protected Jesus from King Herod by taking his family into Egypt and, when King Herod died, he took them back home to Nazareth.

You could explain that Joseph went on to look after Jesus as if he were his own son. Later on, he taught him how to be a carpenter. Talk about the ways in which Joseph was a true friend to Mary and Jesus by giving them his support and protection. Joseph's Christmas gift was true friendship.

Drama games

Unsung heroes

Explain that the term 'unsung hero' refers to someone who quietly gets on with doing something important, perhaps over a long period of time, with little fuss or reward. Point out that there are many people doing important jobs all around us whom we often take for granted.

Whisper one of the following jobs to a child: postman (or woman); ambulance driver; lollipop lady (or man); dustman (or woman); teacher; vicar. The child mimes the job to the rest of the group. Whoever guesses correctly mimes the next job.

Alternatively, ask everyone to stand in a space. As you call out each job, invite everyone to mime it. Call out ideas for actions if necessary. If anyone is doing a particularly interesting mime, invite everyone else to 'freeze', to watch him or her for a short time.

Follow-up discussion

Chat together about some of the jobs that the children mimed. What would happen if no one did that job? Could Joseph be called an unsung hero? What would have happened if Joseph had not given his care and protection to Mary and Jesus?

Stress the importance of people in support roles, such as a veterinary nurse, a football coach and a school secretary. How would the vet, the football team and the head teacher cope without them? If there is time, ask the children to talk with a partner for a few minutes about someone they know whom they consider to be an unsung hero. Would anyone like to tell the group about this person?

Handle with care!

Invite everyone to stand in a circle. Explain that they are going to mime passing round an object that needs careful handling, such as a plate of wobbly jelly, a lighted candle, a baby, an expensive glass vase, or a lively hamster. Give the imaginary object to the person next to you. Say what the object is and explain in each case that everyone needs to watch that the jelly doesn't wobble off the plate, the candle doesn't blow out and so on.

Encourage everyone to take his or her time, to try to be as realistic as possible, and to have some fun with the hamster!

Follow-up discussion

Chat together about things that need careful handling, including our friendships. Talk about the need to work at keeping our friendships good and strong. Think about internet social networking sites and whether all of the people we are in touch with could really be called 'friends'. If not, what is the difference between a small number of true friends and a large number of contacts?

Group craft

You will need

Strips of white paper, all the same size; sticky tape; pencils; crayons; felt-tipped pens

To make friendship paper chains, everyone decorates the paper strips with hearts, drawings of themselves and their friends, or anything related to activities that they enjoy with friends, such as footballs, bikes, skateboards and so on. Bend one strip into a circle and stick the ends together. As each person finishes a strip, help him or her to thread it through the previous one until you have a long chain.

Ask each child about his or her drawing. Display the chains over a noticeboard in your meeting place as a symbol of the friendship of the entire group. You might like to encourage the group to support one another in keeping up their church or midweek club activities.

Individual craft

You will need

A4 pieces of white card with a simple outline of Joseph drawn on them, such as a large triangle with a rounded top, leaving room for the children to draw long arms and hands on either side (one per child); pencils; crayons; glue; Christmas napkins (optional)

To make a napkin holder, ask the children to draw two long, outstretched arms with mitten shapes on the ends, on their Joseph outlines (or you could draw them in advance). Next, draw Joseph's face and clothes and colour them in. Cut out the figure of Joseph and bend the arms around in front, gluing the two hands together. The children can experiment with folding a napkin so that it fits inside Joseph's arms and the holder stands up.

Craft in pairs

You will need

Identical lengths of different coloured string, raffia or ribbon for tying up presents

Invite the children to have fun in pairs, twisting the different coloured lengths together to make festive ties. The lengths should be knotted at one end and held by one child as the other twists or plaits the colours together. Finish with another knot. The strings could be taken home to tie up a present for someone special.

If you are planning to perform the presentation on pages 65–70, reserve some ties for the performance.

Prayer

Chat together about how Christmas is about celebrating Jesus' birth. What might some people think that Christmas is all about? Suggestions might include shopping; parties; overeating; fashion; getting new things. Is the real meaning of Christmas in danger of being forgotten? Does Christmas need to be protected?

In what ways did Joseph take care of his family? How can we take care of the Christmas story and remind people what happened? Ideas might include sending Christmas cards with a nativity scene on them; making nativity Christmas decorations; reading a nativity story to younger brothers and sisters; inviting relations to a carol service at school or church.

Dear God, thank you for Joseph, who quietly gave his support and protection to Mary and Jesus. This was his Christmas gift. Please help us to follow his example by working hard at being a true friend to others. We know that many people today do not know the Christmas story and that it is in danger of being forgotten. Please help us to think of ways in which we could protect the Christmas story this year… [pause]. *Thank you for listening to our ideas. Amen*

Party bag

Give each child a spare card from the individual craft so that he or she can take it home to use as a template over the coming week, or in the Christmas holidays, to make a full set of nativity napkin holders for the Christmas table. Encourage everyone to tell the nativity story to their families on Christmas Day.

★

The shepherds

Theme
Being watchful

Bible story
Luke 2:8–20

Ready, steady...

Despite all the people of wealth and rank at the time, God chose
to reveal his newborn Son to humble shepherds. Thanks to the
census, Bethlehem was crammed full of people on the night Jesus
was born, yet most were oblivious of the miraculous event taking
place. Many slept through it and didn't catch a glimpse of bright
angels or hear a snatch of heavenly music, but the shepherds living
out in the nearby fields missed out on nothing. They were wide
awake because they were keeping watch over their flocks of sheep
and goats. These animals were greatly prized for the wool, meat
and milk that they provided. Goats' milk was used to make cheese,
butter and yoghurt. Even the horns of the sheep were used as
containers for oil.

Perhaps the sheep were soon to be sold in Jerusalem, just six
miles away, where they might be used as offerings at the temple.
In this case, they had to be in excellent condition, with no cuts
or tears to their legs or ears. No wonder a shepherd kept a good
lookout for wild animals on the attack or a sheep caught in a
bramble. (The young David rescued his sheep from a lion and

a bear before God guided him to become the shepherd of his people.)

The Bible often uses the idea of a shepherd to convey the degree of care with which God looks after his people (see, for example, Psalm 23; Isaiah 40:11; Ezekiel 34:11–16). In John 10:1–18, Jesus refers to himself as 'the good shepherd' who knows his own sheep by name and is willing to lay down his life for them. In Luke 15:3–7, he tells the story of a lost sheep and the lengths to which a good shepherd will go to find it. Perhaps this is why God chose shepherds to be the first witnesses of the baby in the manger. These men, who led such a simple life outdoors, would have felt quite at home in a humble stable. Their lack of status did not prevent them from understanding the enormous significance of the event—a Saviour who was born for them.

Society today puts pressure on us to celebrate Christmas in elaborate ways, yet there is a great joy to be found in simple activities. For example, families might enjoy a home-made game at Christmas, such as setting out four simple tasks in four different areas of the house for everyone to complete individually. Fifteen minutes could be allocated for each task before moving on to the next. The tasks could include the ideas below. After the tasks have been completed, everyone could vote on the best entries and a small prize could be given to the winner.

- See how many pieces you can insert in an incomplete jigsaw.
- Decorate a plain biscuit with red and green icing pens (available in supermarkets).
- In silence, write or draw your best or funniest Christmas memories (supply a long roll of wallpaper for this).
- Make up a new Christmas song ready to be performed.

We can all reflect the shepherds' watchfulness by looking out for the real meaning and joy of Christmas in simple activities and acts of giving.

Go!

Once again, display the Christmas present, now with three layers of wrapping remaining. Ask the children how awake they are feeling. When do they feel most lively and alert—in the early morning or late at night? Point out that some people are like larks, ready to rise early, and others are like owls, most active at night.

Ask if it is a good thing to be alert. Has anyone ever fallen asleep in the car on a long journey and missed seeing something special out of the window? Encourage children to tell the group what happened. Be ready with a story of your own in case it is needed. How do we feel when we realise that we have missed out? Point out that while there is nothing wrong with having a good rest, it is also good to be lively, alert and aware of what is going on around us. Mention games such as I-spy. What other observation games do we play? How observant are we?

Icebreaker

You will need

15 white paper circles on a large tray, each representing a sheep: on each circle, draw an oval face with eyes, mouth and two black ears towards the top left; then clearly write a name on each sheep, such as Woolly, Bob, Spot, Bramble, Dozy, Dandelion, Daisy, and so on

Bring out the tray and explain that everyone can look at its contents for one minute only, in complete silence. Start the time. When the time is up, remove the tray and collect up the sheep. Place the empty tray back in front of the children and ask how many sheep there were. What were their names? Invite everyone to take turns to give one name at a time. Put the sheep back on the tray as each one is named, until you have all 15 or as many as can be recalled.

Ask how important it is to notice things. Why is that? Suggestions might include noticing that someone is unwell or unhappy, or that there is a risk of danger.

Dramatised Bible story

Explain that today's Bible story is all about some people who were very good at keeping watch. Invite someone to unwrap the third layer of the Christmas present to reveal the shepherd.

Explain that on the night when Jesus was born, there were shepherds living out in the fields, keeping watch over their flocks. (It would be useful to show a picture of some shepherds from a book or Christmas card at this point.) Talk about the ways in which a shepherd had to use his eyes and ears to look after his sheep and keep them safe. Examples might include looking out for wild animals that might attack (such as lions, bears, jackals and hyenas); looking out for green grass for the sheep to eat, fresh water (in a stream or well) for them to drink, any sheep with injuries needing attention, or some shelter for the flock at night (such as a cave).

Background to the story

A shepherd would typically have been a tough man, used to spending his entire time outdoors. He sometimes slept at the entrance to a cave, where his sheep were sheltered, in order to protect them from wild animals. He carried a heavy club spiked with sharp stones to beat off wild animals, and a leather sling for throwing stones to frighten animals away. He also carried a staff, which he used as a walking stick in rough country and also to control his sheep.

Invite everyone to close their eyes and to picture the scene out in the fields near Bethlehem. Perhaps the shepherds are sitting around

a fire, trying to keep warm and telling each other stories to keep
themselves awake. Perhaps some are eating their supper of bread
and cheese, which they have brought in a leather bag. A few lights
shine in the town of Bethlehem. Stars twinkle in the inky blue sky.
It is a night just like any other… or is it?

Before you read the story together, ask the children to listen
carefully to discover what it was that terrified these tough men, and
what amazing thing they found in a very unexpected place. The
story can be divided among several children.

Narrator 1:	That night in the fields near Bethlehem, some shepherds were guarding their sheep.
Narrator 2:	All at once, an angel came down to them from the Lord, and the brightness of the Lord's glory flashed around them.
Narrator 3:	The shepherds were frightened. But the angel said…
Angel:	Don't be afraid! I have good news for you, which will make everyone happy. This very day in King David's home town a Saviour was born for you. He is Christ the Lord. You will know who he is, because you will find him dressed in baby clothes and lying on a bed of hay.
Narrator 1:	Suddenly many other angels came down from heaven and joined in praising God. They said…
All:	Glory to God in heaven! Peace on earth to everyone who pleases God.
Narrator 2:	After the angels had left and gone back to heaven, the shepherds said to each other…
Shepherd:	Let's go to Bethlehem and see what the Lord has told us about.

Reproduced with permission from *Seasonal Activities for Christmas Festivities* by Vicki Howie (BRF/Barnabas, 2012)
www.barnabasinchurches.org.uk

Narrator 3:	They hurried off and found Mary and Joseph, and they saw the baby lying on a bed of hay.
Narrator 1:	When the shepherds saw Jesus, they told his parents what the angel had said about him.
Narrator 2:	Everyone listened and was surprised. But Mary kept thinking about all this and wondering what it meant.
Narrator 3:	As the shepherds returned to their sheep, they were praising God and saying wonderful things about him.
Narrator 1:	Everything they had seen and heard was just as the angel had said.

Follow-up discussion

Chat about the shepherds being frightened by the appearance of the angel, and about how they found Jesus lying on a bed of hay. Of all the important people God could have chosen to tell about the birth of his Son, why did he choose simple shepherds?

There is no right answer, but suggestions might include the fact that God wanted to show that Jesus was born for ordinary people such as you and me. Perhaps he wanted to show that we don't have to pass lots of exams to understand the Christmas message that Jesus is God's Son and was born to be our friend. Perhaps it was because he was sending Jesus to us to look after us with great care.

The shepherds were awake in a quiet place on the hillside outside busy Bethlehem, so they were very much aware of the angels. Perhaps God wants us to make some quiet time in our busy lives to be aware of what he might be saying to us.

Point out that the Bible says that Jesus knows each of us by name, just as a shepherd would have known all of his sheep by name. God wants us to follow Jesus and trust him to give us all that we need. Wonder together about whether the shepherds might have missed the angels if they hadn't been so watchful. The shepherds' Christmas gift was their watchfulness.

Drama game

Chat about how we are aware of everything happening around us through the five senses. We see with our eyes, we hear with our ears, we feel with nerves in our skin, we taste with the taste buds on our tongues and we smell with our noses.

Choose five children to pretend to be five shepherds from the Bible story, representing sight, sound, touch, taste and smell. Ask the five shepherds to think about the scene on the hillside just before the appearance of the angel. What might each shepherd have seen, heard, felt, tasted and touched? Encourage the children to use their imagination, taking it in turns to add to the picture until they run out of ideas. For example:

Sight: I looked up and I saw many stars twinkling in the sky.

Sound: I heard a lion roaring in the distance.

Touch: I felt the warmth of the fire on my face.

Taste: I found my supper in my bag and I tasted some bread and goat's cheese—delicious!

Smell: I smelled the wood burning on the fire.

Next, ask five different children to describe what, as shepherds, they might have experienced when they arrived in the stable. For example:

Sight: I saw dirt and straw and I saw a newborn baby lying in the manger.

Sound: I heard the baby cry—perhaps he was cold.

Touch: I felt the stony ground under my knees when I knelt down beside him.

Taste: I tasted some dust that blew into my mouth.

Smell: I smelled warm, wet fur and sweet, dry hay.

Encourage everyone to be creative. If anyone is stuck, ask the rest of the group to help out with ideas, but encourage the shepherds to repeat the idea so that they feel that they have successfully completed the task.

Follow-up discussion

Chat together about whether it is surprising that Jesus, the Son of God, was born in a simple stable. The first Christmas was very simple, so how might God feel about all the amazing presents, food and entertainment that we expect to have at Christmas today? Are these elaborate things what Christmas is really all about? Would they please God?

What might be some simple ways to celebrate Christmas that would please God? Suggestions might include giving the gift of our time, perhaps by visiting a lonely neighbour; giving less expensive presents, perhaps seeing what could be bought with just a small amount of money; giving simple home-made presents, such as biscuits or sweets; giving the gift of our company to our families, rather than playing on a computer.

Group craft

You will need

An old roll of wallpaper; pencils; crayons; felt-tipped pens

41

Unroll a long stretch of wallpaper along a table. Invite everyone to draw pictures or write about some simple activities that they have enjoyed at past Christmases or might try out this Christmas. Add one or two examples in advance, such as, 'I decorated some biscuits with red, white and green icing' accompanied by a drawing of some biscuits decorated with holly or Christmas trees.

As the children decorate the paper, discuss together what was so enjoyable about the activities they are drawing. Think about the ways in which our relationships are more important than material possessions.

Individual craft

Flying angel

You will need

Rectangles of white card about the size of a postcard (one per child); short pieces of string (two per child); pencils; a hole punch

Ask the children to draw a simple flying angel on one side of the card and then turn the card over and draw stars all over the other side. Punch a hole in the middle of each short edge and tie string through each hole. Show the children how to roll the string quickly between the fingers and thumbs of each hand so that the card twists over and over, making the angel appear to fly in the sky.

Shepherds' gift wrap

> ### You will need
>
> Sheets of brown paper wrapping (one per child); felt-tipped pens; Christmas stickers

Christmas presents can look very simple and attractive wrapped in brown paper and tied with string or raffia. Invite the children to add one or two Christmassy drawings (for instance, a robin on a postbox or a bunch of holly) in central areas of the paper. The decorated paper could be taken home to wrap a present for someone special.

If you are planning to perform the presentation on pages 65–70, you might like to reserve some wrapping for the performance.

Prayer

Just as the watchful shepherds heard God speaking to them (through the angels), so we need to be alert to what he might be saying to us. Perhaps there is something he wants us to do or understand. Explain that we may not hear God's actual voice or the voices of angels, but God might put a thought into our minds as we spend some quiet time each day thinking about what he wants to say to us, or as we read a book, listen to music, look at a picture or talk to a good friend.

Dear God, thank you for the watchful shepherds and for all the wonderful things that they saw and heard that first Christmas. Their watchfulness was their Christmas gift. Please put some thoughts and ideas into our minds about simple things we could do for other people this Christmas that would really please you… (pause). Please help us to practise being quiet for a few moments every day so that we can be alert to what you want to say to us. Amen

Party bag

Invite everyone to try to spend some quiet time every day this week, talking to God and listening out for his voice. Perhaps they could share next week how they managed to find some quiet moments. Perhaps it will be when they first wake up in the morning, or perhaps it will be last thing at night. They might like to take home one of the sheep from the icebreaker game as a reminder to do this. Explain that, just as a sheep knows the voice of his shepherd, so we can start to recognise God's voice in our lives.

Alternatively, ask everyone to think up an all-age game for their families to play this Christmas. Their ideas could be given out after the presentation or included in your church magazine.

The wise men

> ## Theme
> Having a sense of wonder
>
> ## Bible story
> Matthew 2:1–12

Ready, steady...

People often assume that faith and science represent two contradictory ways of thinking, but the story of the wise men shows us that science and faith can dovetail to lead us to the truth. At the time of Jesus' birth, the Jewish people had been waiting more than 400 years for a promised king. Learned men in distant countries had also heard tales of a king who would be sent by God. In those days, scientists studied the stars and planets and, with much painstaking work, were able to make accurate charts of their movements. They believed that they could learn about the future from these charts and so they were thought of as 'wise men'. When Jesus was born, astrologers noted a new and particularly bright star shining in the eastern sky. There are various possible explanations for this: it may have been a planetary conjunction or a long-tailed comet with the head pointing to Bethlehem and therefore appearing to stand over the place where Jesus was born.

The wise men wondered at the star, decided that it heralded the birth of the promised king and set off with real purpose from their country (probably Arabia, Mesopotamia or Persia) to Jerusalem to ask for the newborn king. It was a journey of one or two months' duration. Herod managed to disguise his horror, and his religious teachers sent them to Bethlehem, the birthplace foretold by the prophet Micah. By the time the wise men reached Bethlehem, Mary and Joseph must have moved to a simple house. Here the travellers knelt to worship the baby clasped in his mother's arms, certain that they had found the long-awaited king.

It is a wonderful thing that the Christian faith encourages us to ask questions and seek out the truth (Matthew 7:7–9). We are not asked to believe blindly. Read Matthew 2:1–12, noting how the wise men's scientific knowledge, coupled with their faith and determination, led them to Jesus.

What things in the natural world fill you with wonder? How might we be encouraged to sit still and simply wonder about the things around us? God spoke to the wise men through a star, something that was of great interest to astrologers. God often speaks to us through our individual passions, but we need to know what these are. How might we best find out where our interests and talents lie?

Go!

Display the Christmas present, now with two layers of wrapping remaining. Start by telling the children about something you have seen in the natural world that was wonderful, such as the peaks of snowy mountains above the clouds, seen from an aeroplane, a huge wave breaking on a surfers' beach or a very large spider's web glistening with dew. Explain that it filled you with wonder. Chat together about what the word 'wonder' means. One definition might be 'surprise mingled with admiration or curiosity'. Does this sum it up? What things have the children seen in the natural world that filled them with wonder? Why was that? Wonder together at how everything was made, but don't draw any conclusions.

Icebreaker

You will need

Five 'mystery' pictures, cut from gardening, wildlife or nature magazines in such a way as to show only part of some natural objects (examples might include part of a coral reef, a close-up of a raindrop or petal, the eye of an animal, the glow of a star and so on); pencils; paper

Place the five cuttings around the room and number them. Ask the children, perhaps in pairs, to wander around the room studying the pictures and writing down what they think each picture shows. Allow plenty of time for the children to wonder and to discuss ideas with each other.

After the allotted time, chat about what everyone has written. Next, give the answers and talk about being curious to find out what the pictures showed. Is it a good thing to be curious about things and to wonder? Why is that? One suggestion might be that wondering makes us think and ask questions, and asking questions helps us to find out about things. Point out that scientists study our world in order to learn more about it. Are any of the children interested in science? What do they enjoy about it?

Dramatised Bible story

Explain that today's Bible story is all about some people who wondered about a natural object that led them to Jesus. Choose someone to unwrap the next layer of the Christmas present to reveal the wise men. Explain that we don't know very much about the wise men. However, we do know that they were scientists who studied the stars and the planets. Explain that they must have gazed at all the stars in the night sky over and over again and wondered why they moved in certain ways. With a lot of hard work, they measured the positions of the stars every night and then made wonderful maps or charts showing the paths they took in the sky. This must have taken them many years of hard work, watching and drawing everything they observed.

Before you read the story together, ask the children to listen carefully to discover what made the wise men think that a new king had been born and what question the wise men asked in Jerusalem. The storytelling can be divided among several children.

Narrator 1:   When Jesus was born in the village of Bethlehem in Judea, Herod was king. During this time some wise men from the east came to Jerusalem and said…

Wise man 1: Where is the child born to be king of the Jews?

Wise man 2: We saw his star in the east…

Wise man 3: and have come to worship him.

Narrator 2:   When King Herod heard about this, he was worried, and so was everyone else in Jerusalem.

Narrator 3:   Herod brought together the chief priests and the teachers of the Law of Moses and asked them…

Herod: Where will the Messiah be born?

Narrator 1:   They told him…

Teacher 1:   He will be born in Bethlehem, just as the prophet wrote…

Teacher 2:   'Bethlehem in the land of Judea, you are very important among the towns of Judea.'

Teacher 3:   'From your town will come a leader, who will be like a shepherd for my people Israel.'

Reproduced with permission from *Seasonal Activities for Christmas Festivities* by Vicki Howie (BRF/Barnabas, 2012)
www.barnabasinchurches.org.uk

Narrator 2:	Herod secretly called in the wise men and asked them when they had first seen the star. He told them…
Herod:	Go to Bethlehem and search carefully for the child. As soon as you find him, let me know. I want to go and worship him, too.
Narrator 3:	The wise men listened to what the king said and then left.
Narrator 1:	And the star they had seen in the east went on ahead of them until it stopped over the place where the child was. They were thrilled and excited to see the star.
Narrator 2:	When the men went into the house and saw the child with Mary, his mother, they knelt down and worshipped him.
Narrator 3:	They took out their gifts of gold, frankincense and myrrh and gave them to him. Later they were warned in a dream not to return to Herod, and they went back home by another road.

Follow-up discussion

Chat about how the wise men saw a new star in the sky and thought that it must be the sign that a new king had been born. Talk about how they asked where the new king was: they probably thought he would be at the palace. Chat together about what would have happened if the wise men had not wondered at the star and set out on their long journey. If they had not asked such a bold question, they might not have found the baby Jesus. So perhaps the wise men's Christmas gift was their sense of wonder. Stress that it is important to wonder, to ask questions and then to be determined to find the answers.

Reproduced with permission from *Seasonal Activities for Christmas Festivities* by Vicki Howie (BRF/Barnabas, 2012)
www.barnabasinchurches.org.uk

Drama game

Explain that, after the wise men had seen the star, they must have set out with great determination on their journey. They didn't know exactly where they were going or how long it would take them to find the new king, but they had great faith that they would find him. Talk about the disappointments or setbacks they might have had on the way, such as not finding Jesus at the palace and having still further to go to Bethlehem. Did they give up? No, they kept going. They had great perseverance.

Ask the children to find a partner and to sit down at some distance from the other pairs. Explain that you are going to ask everyone to talk to their partner for one minute about a hobby, interest, ambition or job they would like to do when they are older. It should be something they feel really enthusiastic about. Give everyone time to think and discuss what their topics might be.

Before they begin, explain that you want both members of each pair to talk to each other at the same time but without shouting. Point out that this will be distracting but that they must try to concentrate on their own topics and keep going throughout the minute. Wander around, listening in and encouraging everyone to keep going. At the end, congratulate those who managed to persevere.

Follow-up discussion

Ask whether the children found the exercise easy. If not, why not? Chat about times when we might get distracted, such as when we are trying to do some homework, practising music or doing a job. How might we overcome being distracted? Ideas might include keeping going until a certain time, not putting the television on until the work is done, switching off a mobile phone, keeping going for five minutes and then another five minutes, and so on.

Chat together about other reasons for giving up on something, and think of ways of overcoming them. For example, if a task is too difficult, we could ask a friend, family member or teacher for some help; if it's too boring, we could keep going a little longer and it may become more interesting; we could work towards a reward, such as a favourite television programme, or work in small bursts, one step at a time.

Is it easier to keep going with something that we enjoy? If so, perhaps this is a sign (remember, the star was a sign) of a talent we have.

If there is time, play other 'perseverance' games, such as a team relay race, seeing how many times a pair can throw and catch a ball or beanbag, or seeing how long everyone can keep a Christmas balloon in the air by patting it to each other.

The wise men were filled with wonder when they saw the bright new star. They set out with determination to find the new king and they didn't turn back until they had reached their goal. Their journey took them closer and closer to Jesus.

Group craft

You will need

Rolls of crêpe paper; scissors; sticky tape; glue; tinsel; glitter; paper streamers

Make a long Christmas frieze for your venue with a pattern that keeps going. Give the children strips of crêpe paper, loosely rolled and then flattened. Ask them to cut semi-circles (planets) and half-star shapes from the folded edges. Unroll the strips of crêpe paper and tape them together. Decorate the frieze and stick on cut paper streamers to hang from the bottom edge.

Individual craft

You will need

Sheets of thin white paper (one per child); star stamps or sponges; different-coloured ink pads or paint

Invite everyone to have fun printing their own 'star of wonder' wrapping paper. The paper could be taken home to wrap a present for someone special.

If you are planning to perform the presentation on pages 65–70, you might like to keep some of the wrapping for the performance.

Prayer

Chat together about how our lives are like journeys. In what ways might the wise men in our story inspire us? Suggestions might include wondering, asking questions and finding out about things; setting ourselves goals to achieve and not being put off by setbacks or distractions; being determined; looking out for signs of our talents.

Chat about how the wise men's journey took them closer and closer to Jesus. Would this be a good goal for us? If so, how could we try to get to know Jesus better every day? For example, perhaps we could ask ourselves questions about Jesus, wonder about what he teaches us and try to find the answers by praying every day. We could read Bible stories, attend church groups and services, or spend time admiring God's wonderful world and generally puzzling things out.

Dear God, thank you for the wise men's sense of wonder. This was their Christmas gift. Thank you that you used something they were interested in—a bright new star—to lead them to Jesus. Please help us to look out for signs of our own talents and to keep going at improving them. Help us to keep asking questions about you and your wonderful world and to keep searching until we find the truth. Amen

Party bag

Give the children a simple star shape to decorate at home and display in their bedrooms as a reminder to keep going towards a particular goal. Alternatively, in the coming week, the children could write down five things that they have wondered at or about, on the five points of the star.

★

Jesus

> **Theme**
> Giving the gift of love
>
> **Bible story**
> Luke 2:1–7; John 3:16

Ready, steady...

God did not send his Son into the world to condemn it, but to save it through him (John 3:16–17). It was an act of selfless love, quite undeserved by us, which shone light into a dark world. Wherever he went, Jesus showed people God's love. He met people where they were, not just physically but emotionally and spiritually, and they responded to his friendship and love by becoming better people. Love is a powerful force, as the story of Zacchaeus shows (Luke 19:1–10).

Unfortunately, at this busy time of year, we are apt to forget about love as we anxiously count down the number of shopping days left until Christmas. We forget 'the reason for the season' and think of Christmas as a date rather than as a state of mind. It could be Christmas every day if we did the little loving things for other people that we know would please God, instead of striving for 'the perfect Christmas' just once a year.

In Luke 12:22–32, Jesus tells his disciples not to worry about material things such as food and clothes. Instead, if we seek God's kingdom by putting love into action, then all these things will be given to us as well. Even when we know that Jesus is God's gift to us, it is good to think more deeply to discover what this really means. How can a person be a gift? How can we explain to others that Jesus is love? What stories do we know about Jesus that show his loving attitude?

Many of us have difficulty in giving up a favourite thing for someone else, but how much God must love us to have given up something as precious as his only Son. Often we have trouble putting ourselves in another's shoes. How might we take time in a busy schedule to help others? Some people are easier to love than others. This is a normal feeling, but it is easier to love others when we look at them with God's eyes and let his love flow through us. To be able to do this, we need to know with confidence that God loves us; his gift of love needs to be accepted or received by us before we can show it to others.

Go!

Display the Christmas present, now with just one layer of wrapping remaining. Start by telling the children about a parcel that you may have received through the post. Explain that the postman rang the bell and that you had to check the name on the parcel and then sign for it. Say what it turned out to be.

Chat about the sort of parcels we like to receive. Do we like big parcels or small ones? Soft and squidgy or a firm box shape? Do we prefer to give a present or to receive one?

Icebreaker

You will need

Some different-coloured jelly babies or a variety of biscuits wrapped in Christmas paper (enough for each child)

Ask everyone to think of, but not to say out loud at this stage, five things that we do when someone gives us a present. Allow a short time for thought. Next, explain that you are going to give one of the children a present. Invite everyone to see whether the things that they thought of actually happen. The conversation and actions need to bring in the five elements of receiving, unwrapping, saying 'thank you', enjoying and sharing. For example:

Leader: As it's nearly Christmas (child's name), I've
             brought you a small gift. Shut your eyes and open
             your hands!

Child: What have I done to deserve this?

Leader: Just being yourself!

Child: Oh, how exciting! (She receives the gift.) What
             lovely paper!

Leader: Aren't you going to open it?

Child: Can I unwrap it now, then?

Leader: Of course you can!

Child: Here we go, then! (She partly unwraps the gift and
             peers into the paper so that no one else sees the gift.)
             Oh, my favourites! Thank you very much indeed!

Leader: I think the others want to see.

Child: Oh, sorry! Look, I've got some jelly babies [or
             biscuits]. I love these! In fact, I think I'm going to
             have one now. (She pops one in her mouth.) Mmm,
             delicious! (She makes a big show of enjoying it.)

Leader: You're making us all want one now!

Child: Well, you can! Here, I'll share them round. (She
             does so.)

Reproduced with permission from *Seasonal Activities for Christmas Festivities* by Vicki Howie (BRF/Barnabas, 2012)
www.barnabasinchurches.org.uk

Follow-up discussion

When everyone has finished their treat, chat about the five words or phrases. Talk about everyone's favourite and least favourite coloured sweet or type of biscuit. Which would be the most difficult to give away? Why is that? What might encourage us to give our favourite away to someone else? What is the difference between being selfish and being selfless?

Dramatised Bible story

Recap the various people involved in the nativity story and what each of them gave at the first Christmas. Explain that today you are thinking about what the Christmas gift was—and still is. Ask someone to unwrap the last layer to reveal baby Jesus. Talk about how he is God's gift to us: he is the reason for the season.

Before you read the story together, ask the children to listen carefully to discover what reason God had for giving us such a precious gift. The storytelling can be divided among several children.

Narrator 1:   About that time, the Emperor Augustus gave orders for the names of all the people to be listed in record books.

Narrator 2:   Everyone had to go to their own home town to be listed, so Joseph had to leave Nazareth in Galilee and go to Bethlehem in Judea.

Narrator 3:   Long ago, Bethlehem had been King David's home town, and Joseph went there because he was from David's family.

Narrator 4:   Mary was engaged to Joseph and travelled with him to Bethlehem.

Reproduced with permission from *Seasonal Activities for Christmas Festivities* by Vicki Howie (BRF/Barnabas, 2012)
www.barnabasinchurches.org.uk

Narrator 5:   She was soon going to have a baby and, while they were there, she gave birth to her firstborn son.

Narrator 6:   She dressed him in baby clothes and laid him in a bed of hay, because there was no room for them in the inn.

Pause.

Narrator 7:   God loved the people of this world so much that he gave his only Son, so that everyone who has faith in him will have eternal life and never really die.

Follow-up discussion

Chat together about the ways in which this short report of Jesus' birth differs from reports today about a royal birth or the birth of a celebrity's baby. Talk about how Jesus came to be one of us so that he could experience all the things in life that we do. He came to share all our ups and downs. He understands how we feel because he too lived in our world. God gave us his only Son because he loves us so much.

Would it have been hard for God to part with Jesus and let him be born into the world? Why or why not? Talk about how God acted selflessly out of his great love for us. He wanted Jesus to come into the world to tell us how much God loves us. Chat about how we can try to reflect God's gift of love by having a loving attitude towards others.

Reproduced with permission from *Seasonal Activities for Christmas Festivities* by Vicki Howie (BRF/Barnabas, 2012)
www.barnabasinchurches.org.uk

Drama games

Christmas mix and match

You will need

Five pieces of paper or card, each with one of the following written on it: receive; unwrap; say thank you; enjoy; share

Recap the five things we do with a Christmas present and show the words. Remind the children that Jesus is our Christmas present from God and talk about the ways in which the different nativity characters did the things on the cards. As you do so, invite children to place each character on the appropriate card, as below. (You may find that some characters could be placed on more than one card.) The word 'share' will be left. Chat about how we can all share the good news about Jesus by telling everyone we meet about the true meaning of Christmas. After the activity, you might like to invite the children to arrange all the characters in a nativity scene.

- Mary was willing to receive the gift of Jesus into her life and her home. (*Place Mary on the word 'receive'.*)
- Just as we unwrap a gift to find out what we have been given, the wise men wondered about the star and wanted to unwrap the meaning behind it. (*Place the wise man on the word 'unwrap'.*)
- The watchful shepherds said 'thank you' to God by praising God for all the things they had seen and heard on the hillside and in the stable. (*Place a shepherd on the words 'say thank you'.*)
- Joseph enjoyed taking care of Mary and Jesus. (*Place Joseph on the word 'enjoy'.*)
- We have our own part to play in the Christmas story as we share the good news of Jesus' birth with others. (*Gather together around the crib scene.*)

Christmas charades

Divide the children into five small groups. Explain that each group is going to create and rehearse a very short and simple mini-play lasting only about 30 seconds, to perform to the others. Allocate one of the themes below to each group.

- Getting ready for some Christmas visitors and welcoming them into your home.
- Going into a bookshop or library to buy or borrow a nativity storybook to read.
- Going carol singing with some friends on a cold and frosty evening.
- Getting ready for bed on Christmas Eve, including hanging up a stocking and saying a prayer.
- Telling a friend at school about a Christmas activity at your church club and inviting them to come along.

Give the children a few moments to think up their stories and help them with some ideas. Invite each group to perform their mini-story, explaining that you realise they haven't had time to rehearse properly, but that this is part of the fun. Applaud each group's work. After each one, you might like to make the following points.

- We receive the gift of Jesus into our lives and homes whenever we are willing to do things that would please him, including welcoming visitors into our homes.
- We unwrap the gift of Jesus whenever we wonder about him and make the effort to find out more about him—for instance, by reading a storybook or listening to a talk about him at church.
- We say 'thank you' to God for the gift of Jesus whenever we sing carols and think about the words we are singing.
- We enjoy the gift of our friendship with Jesus whenever we spend time getting to know him by talking with him in prayer—at bedtime, for instance, or at any time.

- We share the gift of Jesus by telling others about him and explaining that he is God's gift to everyone.

Put yourself in my shoes!

Ask the children to spread out around the room. Announce various types of footwear, such as high heels, flippers, rollerskates, stilts and so on. Ask the children to spend a moment or two imagining what these items of footwear are like, such as the colour, whether the heels are high or low, whether the toes are rounded or pointed, and so on. Are they comfortable to wear?

The children now mime putting on the different items and walking around the room in them. After a while, call out various obstacles for everyone to negotiate, such as a flight of steps, a steep slope up and down, a river to wade into and swim across, a room with a low ceiling, a slippery floor and so on.

Follow-up discussion

Discuss the different types of footwear. Did the children find some easier to walk in than others? Which obstacles were difficult for which types of footwear? Were they easier in another type of footwear?

Next, chat about everyday life. Is it true that one person finds something easy while another finds it difficult? Why could that be? If we can do something easily, do we find it difficult to understand why someone else has trouble with it? How good are we at putting ourselves in someone else's shoes? (You might need to explain what this means.) In what ways might we have a more kindly attitude to others if we tried putting ourselves in that person's shoes?

Pass it on!

> ### You will need
>
> An old ball or beanbag with a heart or the word 'Love' drawn or written on it

Play a simple game of catch and pass the ball. After a while, introduce an ever-shorter time restriction on holding the ball or beanbag. Anyone who drops it is out. Use the game to point out that God loves us so much that he gave away what was most precious to him—his only Son. When we really believe and understand that God loves us, we receive his gift of love and that helps us to be more loving and giving to others.

When we don't feel like forgiving others, it is helpful to remember that God forgives us and carries on loving us even though we don't deserve it. Perhaps we should do the same for others. Stress that it is easier to forgive others if we do it quickly rather than letting a grudge build up.

Group craft

> ### You will need
>
> **Savoury items** such as small, long brown rolls, cut in half lengthways (*manger*), grated carrot or strips of yellow pepper (*hay*), small cocktail sausages or gherkins (*baby*), sliced carrot, sliced stuffed olives or rounds of thin cheese (*halo*); **sweet items** such as a bowl of rice cereal mixed with melted chocolate (*manger*), strawberry shoelaces (*hay*), a jelly baby (*baby*), white and yellow icing pens (*halo*)

Let the children have fun making their own sweet or savoury babies in mangers. As they do so, chat together about the different tastes of the foods and link them to the sweet and bitter aspects of Jesus' life. For example:

• He grew up with loving parents.
• He loved learning about God.
• He had good friends.
• He loved meeting people, telling them about God and making them well.

But...

• People often rejected him or didn't believe that he was the Son of God.
• One of his friends betrayed him.
• At Easter, he gave the greatest gift of all, his own life, when he died on the cross in order to open the doors of heaven to all his friends. That is love!

Individual craft

You will need

Folded pieces of thin white card (one per child); shiny paper; thin ribbon; glue

Make a wrapped-present Christmas card. Ask the children to glue the shiny paper to the front of the card. Glue the ribbon across the length and breadth of the card so that it forms a cross shape. Add a bow where the two lengths of ribbon meet, so that the card resembles a wrapped present.

Chat about how the cross shape links in with Jesus' death on the cross, his selfless act of love towards us, and how the bow links in with the amazing result—that he opened the door of heaven for us. You could turn a noticeboard or even a door into a wrapped parcel decoration by covering it with crêpe paper and adding a ribbon cross shape with a bow.

Prayer

Recap the gifts from each of the sessions: being willing, being a true friend, being watchful, having a sense of wonder, and giving the gift of love. Chat about why it can be difficult to love some people, especially if they have hurt us in some way. How might it be helpful to try to see other people as God sees them? Jesus often helped other people by being their friend. Perhaps we can do the same.

Dear God, thank you for loving us so much that you gave us your only Son to share all our ups and downs. You really put yourself in our shoes. Please help us to understand how much you love us. Help us to accept your gift of love so that we, in turn, can be loving to other people. When others are difficult to love, please help us to see them through your eyes and try to be a friend to them. Amen

Party bag

Give each child a heart shape cut out of thin red card. This could be decorated at home and displayed as a reminder of how much God loves us and wants us to love others, too.

If you are planning to perform the presentation on pages 65–70, you might like to reserve some heart shapes for the performance.

★

Christmas unwrapped

Narrator 1:   Happy Christmas, everyone! Christmas is a time for giving.

A wrapped Christmas present is brought on and placed on display.

Child 1:   Thanks very much!

Child 2:   Wow!

Child 3:   Look at that!

Child 4:   I wonder what's inside!

Narrator 2:   Christmas is a time for giving because we are reflecting God's great gift to us at the first Christmas.

Narrator 3:   But what should we give each other today?

Narrator 4:   Over the last five weeks we've been looking at the Christmas story.

Narrator 5:   Yes, we've been unwrapping the story layer by layer, week by week.

Narrator 1:   Focusing on the nativity characters…

Narrator 2:   To find out what each of them gave, that first Christmas…

Narrator 3:   And to think how we can reflect their gifts today.

Reproduced with permission from *Seasonal Activities for Christmas Festivities* by Vicki Howie (BRF/Barnabas, 2012)
www.barnabasinchurches.org.uk

Narrator 4:	In the first session, we unwrapped the first layer of the present…
Child 1:	Rustle, rustle!
Child 2:	Crackle, crackle!
Narrator 5:	And out came the nativity figure of Mary.
Narrator 1:	Mary received a surprise visit from the angel Gabriel, who asked if she would be willing to give God some help.
Narrator 2:	God wanted Mary to be the mother of a special baby. What would she say?
Child 1:	Do I have to?
Child 2:	Later, maybe!
Child 3:	I don't really want to!
Child 4:	I'm no good at that!
Narrator 3:	Not at all! Mary loved and trusted God and she soon replied with a joyful…
All:	*(Loudly)* Yes!
Narrator 4:	She said…
Mary:	I am the Lord's servant. Let it happen as you have said!
Narrator 5:	Mary was happy to help God, and so we decided that her Christmas gift was being willing…
All:	Being willing!
Narrator 1:	And we thought of ways to reflect Mary's gift by being willing, too.
Child 1:	Like being willing to lend a hand this Christmas?
All:	Yes!

Pause.

Reproduced with permission from *Seasonal Activities for Christmas Festivities* by Vicki Howie (BRF/Barnabas, 2012)
www.barnabasinchurches.org.uk

Narrator 2: The following week, we unwrapped the second layer of the parcel.

Narrator 3: And discovered a real unsung hero. It was Joseph.

Narrator 4: Joseph did many good things, quietly and with little fuss.

Narrator 5: He gave Mary his wholehearted support and he protected Jesus from King Herod's jealousy.

Narrator 1: He looked after Jesus as if he were his own son.

Narrator 2: So we decided that Joseph's Christmas gift was being a true friend.

All: A true friend!

Narrator 3: And we all thought of ways to reflect Joseph's gift by working hard at being a true friend today.

Child 2: Like writing a Christmas letter to a friend who moved away?

All: Yes!

Pause.

Narrator 4: The following week, we unwrapped the third layer of the present.

Narrator 5: And we found people who were wide awake on the night when Jesus was born.

Narrator 1: They were out in the fields near Bethlehem, watching over their sheep.

Narrator 2: They saw bright angels in the night sky.

Narrator 3: And heard them singing…

All: Praise God in heaven!

Narrator 4: It was the shepherds. Thanks to their watchfulness, they hurried into Bethlehem and found Christmas in a very humble place.

Reproduced with permission from *Seasonal Activities for Christmas Festivities* by Vicki Howie (BRF/Barnabas, 2012)
www.barnabasinchurches.org.uk

Shepherd 1:	I saw the stable…
Shepherd 2:	I smelled the sweet, dry hay…
Shepherd 3:	I heard the baby crying…
Narrator 5:	We decided that the shepherd's gift was being watchful…
All:	Being watchful!
Narrator 1:	And we thought about using our eyes and ears to look for the real meaning of Christmas.
Narrator 2:	Perhaps in simple Christmas activities…
Child 3:	Like enjoying simple games with our families?
All:	Yes!

Pause.

Narrator 4:	The following week, we unwrapped the fourth layer of the present.
Narrator 5:	Inside we found some people who saw an amazing star and wondered about it.
Narrator 1:	They set out on a journey to find some answers.
Wise man 1:	Where is the child born to be king of the Jews?
Wise man 2:	We saw his star in the east…
Wise man 3:	And have come to worship him.
Narrator 2:	The wise men were determined to keep going until they found the truth.
Narrator 3:	Their knowledge of science and their faith brought them to Jesus.
Narrator 4:	We decided that the wise men's gift was having a sense of wonder.
All:	A sense of wonder!
Narrator 5:	And we thought about how we can develop our own sense of wonder this Christmas.

Reproduced with permission from *Seasonal Activities for Christmas Festivities* by Vicki Howie (BRF/Barnabas, 2012)
www.barnabasinchurches.org.uk

Child 3:	Like gazing up at the stars with your mum or dad on a clear night?
All:	Yes!

Pause.

Narrator 1:	Finally, we unwrapped the last present.
Narrator 2:	We already knew who would be inside. It was…
All:	Baby Jesus!
Narrator 3:	Yes, baby Jesus is God's wonderful gift to us— the reason for the season.
Narrator 4:	God loves us so much that he gave away what was most precious to him—his only Son.
Narrator 5:	We thought ahead to Easter time when Jesus gave his own life for us on the cross.
Narrator 1:	So we decided that God's gift to us is his love…
All:	His love!
Narrator 2:	And we thought that we can reflect God's Christmas gift by showing a loving attitude towards others.
Child 4:	Like making up after a quarrel?
All:	Yes!

Pause.

Narrator 3:	Christmas is a time for giving. What should we give today?
Child 1:	How about some selfless love… *(holds up a heart shape).*
Child 2:	All wrapped up with wise men's 'star of wonder' wrapping paper… *(holds up the 'star of wonder' wrapping).*

Reproduced with permission from *Seasonal Activities for Christmas Festivities* by Vicki Howie (BRF/Barnabas, 2012)
www.barnabasinchurches.org.uk

Child 3:   Followed by a layer of shepherd's humble
            brown paper... *(holds up the wrapping paper)*.
Child 4:   All held together safely with Joseph's ties of
            friendship... *(holds up the ties)*.
Mary: And willingly labelled with the words 'Happy
            Christmas!' written on a 'joyful Mary' gift tag.
            (holds up a gift tag).
All: Happy Christmas—and happy giving—
            everyone!

Christmas unpacked

Themes

Best friends; the broken friendship; time to say sorry; Jesus the go-between; for ever friends

★

Introduction

At Christmas, we naturally concentrate on the nativity story itself. Although this is understandable, it does mean that we don't see Christmas in context. When we look at the bigger picture, we can begin to understand the deeper significance of Christmas. In 'Christmas unpacked', we explore the biblical account of God's relationship with his people through the following stories.

- Adam and Eve (best friends)
- Adam and Eve disobey God (the broken friendship)
- John the Baptist (time to say sorry)
- The prodigal son (Jesus the go-between)
- Jesus' crucifixion and resurrection (for ever friends)

As each story is developed through games, discussion, craft and prayer, we see how Christmas celebrates the fulfilment of God's plan to put right our spoilt friendship. We also explore how we might come closer to God, resist temptation, say sorry, become peacemakers and put others first.

A Christmas stocking, symbolising the way that the stories hang together, is prepared in advance, filled with the following wrapped items.

- A friendship bracelet
- A toy snake
- A small mirror and comb set
- A story DVD or book
- A small cross and chain

The stocking should be filled in reverse order, so that the cross is in the toe and the friendship bracelet is the first gift to be found. Before the first session, read John 1:1–18 and familiarise yourself with the material in the programme, including the presentation on pages 120–125, which acts as a summary. Ideally, encourage any helpers to do the same so that everyone is working towards the same goal. Decide whether you are going to perform the presentation, perhaps within a Christmas service, to show the church family what you have been thinking about. You might like to start making any practical arrangements well in advance.

For the group craft sessions, you will need to prepare a long piece of wallpaper by dividing it into five sections, headed with the five session themes (Best friends; The broken friendship; Time to say sorry; Jesus the go-between; For ever friends). This will be used to create a 'big picture' mural over the five weeks of the programme.

Adam and Eve

> ## Theme
> Best friends
>
> ## Bible story
> Genesis 2:4–25

Ready, steady...

The word 'Genesis' means 'beginning'. The book of Genesis is the beginning of the story about God and his ongoing relationship with people. The first eleven chapters tell the story of the world as God intended it to be and the mess that we have made of it. The rest of the Bible tells the story of all that God has done and is still doing to rescue us from that mess.

The creation story is not meant to be a scientific account of how God made the world. What it does tell us is that the world was made with love and care and came about not by accident but by God's will. It also shows that we have a special place within it (see, for example, Psalm 8). God made us in his own image to be in a close relationship with him. Although we are made from the dust of the ground, God himself breathed life into us; we have a God-like quality and therefore an ability to respond to him if we so choose.

Read Genesis 2:4–25, noting the interaction between God and Adam and the very natural relationship between Adam and Eve. This first session aims to help us think about the closeness and ease that we feel with a best friend and uses that as a model to help us forge a closer relationship with God.

Try to answer the questions in the icebreaker for yourself. In what ways might our relationship with someone we are close to have parallels with our relationship with God? When we analyse the process through which God has become our best friend, we may be able to help others to know him better. For example, how have we got to know God well? What things have we found useful that we could pass on to others?

Go!

Display the filled Christmas stocking in a prominent place. Chat about the fact that it isn't long until Christmas. What do we hang up at the ends of our beds on Christmas Eve? Explain that at Christmas time we usually concentrate just on the nativity story itself. There is a good reason for this, as it tells the story of how God planned that his Son, Jesus, would be born into the world at the first Christmas. However, the Christmas story is only a small part of a much bigger story—the story of all the things God has done for us.

Talk about what happens when we read a book. Do we read just a few paragraphs in the middle of a book? Where do we usually start and how do we proceed? The way to understand the entire story is to read the whole book. Similarly, if we stand too close to a picture, we don't always see what it is meant to be; we need to stand back to see the bigger picture.

Talk about how you'll be unpacking the Christmas stocking over the next five weeks. The gifts will help with exploring five stories from the Bible, starting near the beginning and finishing near the end. In this way, we will discover how Christmas fits into the big picture.

Icebreaker

> ### You will need
>
> A flipchart or a big pad of plain paper; a felt-tipped pen or marker pen

Write 'A best friend is…' in big letters at the top of the paper. Ask the children to think in silence about someone they consider to be a best friend. (This could be someone of a different age, such as a grandparent.) Now ask them to think for a few moments about what makes someone a best friend. Write a list of suggestions on the paper. For example, a best friend might be:

- someone we know very well
- someone we feel at ease with
- someone with similar interests to our own
- someone we can trust
- someone we can talk to easily
- someone who respects us and our things
- someone who does not bully us

When you have a long list of ideas, ask everyone to imagine that a best friend is coming to stay with them for the night. What might they do beforehand to make sure that the friend has an enjoyable time? Start a new list on the pad. Suggestions might include making an attractive or interesting place to play (such as a den or tent); preparing some delicious food to eat; making up a bed in the same room; telling the friend when they arrive about anything dangerous (such as a tap with very hot water) or anything that they are not allowed to do for safety reasons (such as playing on a trampoline at the same time as anyone else or without an adult watching). End the icebreaker by pointing out that it can take time to find a best friend, but that it is worth the wait.

Dramatised Bible story

Explain that our first Bible story comes from the first book in the Bible, Genesis. It's the story of Adam and Eve. Invite someone to fish out the first present from the stocking and unwrap it to reveal the friendship bracelet. Encourage the children to wonder what this has to do with the Bible story, but don't give an answer yet.

Before you read the story together, ask the children to listen carefully to see how many friendly things God does for Adam and Eve. You might like to divide into two teams for this, and see which team comes up with the most answers. The storytelling can be divided among several children.

Narrator 1: When God had made the earth and the heavens, he formed a man from the dust of the ground. He breathed the breath of life into his nostrils, and the man, Adam, became a living being.

Narrator 2: God had planted a beautiful garden, called the garden of Eden, as a home for Adam.

Narrator 3: God made all kinds of trees grow there—trees that were pleasing to the eye and good for food.

Narrator 4: In the middle of the garden were two trees; one gave life and the other gave the power to know the difference between right and wrong.

Narrator 5: God asked Adam to cultivate the garden and take care of it. He told him…

Reproduced with permission from *Seasonal Activities for Christmas Festivities* by Vicki Howie (BRF/Barnabas, 2012)
www.barnabasinchurches.org.uk

God: You may eat fruit from any tree in the garden, except the one that has the power to let you decide the difference between right and wrong. If you eat any fruit from that tree, you will die before the day is over.

Narrator 6: Then God said…

God: It is not good for Adam to be alone. I will make a suitable partner for him.

Narrator 6: So God caused Adam to fall into a deep sleep and, while he was sleeping, God took one of his ribs and closed up his side.

Narrator 1: Then God made a woman, Eve, from the rib he had taken out of Adam, and he brought her to him.

Narrator 2: Adam and Eve were both naked, and they were not ashamed.

Narrator 3: Then God brought all the animals and birds that he had made to Adam to see what names he would give each of them. Adam named the tame animals and the birds and the wild animals. That's how they got their names.

Narrator 4: God blessed Adam and Eve and told them to enjoy everything in the world that he had made.

Narrator 5: But although he had put them in charge, they must always obey God.

Narrator 6: This was because God loved them and knew what was best for them.

Follow-up discussion

What friendly things did God do for Adam and Eve? Suggestions might include:

- God blessed Adam and Eve.
- God trusted Adam and Eve to look after everything he had made.
- God gave them plenty of food to choose from.
- God made a beautiful garden for them to look after.
- God warned Adam about the danger of eating from the tree that gave the power to decide the difference between right and wrong.
- God let Adam name all the creatures.
- God made sure that Adam and Eve were not lonely.

Chat together about any similarities between Adam and Eve's relationship with God and the list on the flipchart. Hold up the friendship bracelet. What sort of relationship did God want to have with Adam and Eve? Did he want people to be his best friends?

Drama games

Let's be creative!

This game could be played by the entire group miming each of the phrases below individually, or the children could be divided into groups to devise and then perform their mime to other groups.

Before you start, ask the children if they know what the word 'create' means. Point out that we can make many things, some good and some bad. Either call out the phrases for the children to mime (or act out loud) or let the groups choose a phrase each. It doesn't matter if some groups want to do the same phrase, as it might be interesting to see different interpretations. Whichever you do, be prepared to offer help as needed.

- **Make music:** The children might like to mime playing different instruments, perhaps in an orchestra or small band. You could suggest that someone acts as the conductor. Follow up by chatting together about what orchestra or band members need to do to make a good sound.
- **Make someone smile:** The children could mime being clowns, or different children could take it in turns to tell a favourite joke. Follow up by chatting together about whether or not it is a good thing to make others smile. When might it not be so good to clown around or tell jokes?
- **Make a fuss:** Help everyone to think about the different meanings of this phrase. For instance, the children could act out a scene where a diner in a restaurant makes a fuss about the quality of the food. Perhaps a child makes a fuss because he or she has been told to turn off the television. Perhaps someone makes a fuss of a pet dog. Follow up by chatting together about when it might be a good idea to make a fuss about something and when it might not.
- **Make a masterpiece:** The children could mime painting a portrait, having arranged some sitters into a pleasing group. They might mime sculpting a statue of a famous person, or budding engineers might mime putting a car or engine together. Follow up by chatting together about what makes a piece of work a masterpiece. Has it something to do with the expert craftsmanship, the detail and care, or the beauty of the work? Recap the verse in the Bible story in which God formed the man from dust. In what way could we think of ourselves as being God's masterpieces? God was pleased with everything he made. If God thinks we are wonderful, how should we think of ourselves?
- **Make friends:** You might like to end the game by asking one person to 'make friends' with a second person (perhaps by going up to them, shaking hands and saying 'Hi, I'm…'). The latter responds by saying their name and then makes friends with a

third person, who joins them, and so on until all the children form one large group of friends.

You'll never walk alone!

Ask the children to spread out around the room, and ask if anyone likes going for a walk. Often, it can be more fun to walk with someone—or something—else. Explain that you want everyone to walk with an imaginary person or creature that you are going to call out, and that, whatever happens, you want them to stay alongside this walking partner. As they walk, they should be aware of the rest of the group. They should use the entire space available without bumping into anyone else. Narrate the following instructions.

Wander in a bored fashion around the room… Now you meet an imaginary best friend. Hello! You decide to walk to the park together, so off you go! Your friend walks a bit quicker than you, so keep up… Whoa! Your best friend stops suddenly to tie up a shoelace… Hang on, a bit of trouble with the laces… You jog on the spot while you wait. Oh, now your friend is off at a gentle jog to the park… Keep alongside them but don't get in the way of the other joggers. Stop! Your friend has twisted an ankle… You take a look… Now your friend can only limp through the park and you walk at their slower pace… Now you reach the bench in the park and your friend decides to rest here for a moment.

Look! Here comes a friendly dog. He's on a lead but he seems to have got away from his owner… Hello, dog! You take the lead and begin to take the dog for a walk… Lovely; he walks nicely to heel as you walk briskly, looking out for his owner. Watch out! He suddenly stops to sniff the grass! You wait patiently for a moment… Oh dear, you'll be here all day if you don't pull him on… That's it, he gets going again… But now he keeps pulling on the lead; he's taking you into the undergrowth… He keeps pulling you on. Oh no, he pulls so hard that he gets away from you… You stop and look around.

Wait a minute, what's that coming towards you through the undergrowth? You stare. It can't be, but it is! It's a great, big, beautiful lion! It seems to invite you to walk alongside it as it plants its big, velvety feet on the ground… You take big, soft steps to keep up with this friendly lion. As you do so, you rest your hand on its thick mane. Walking alongside this noble creature, you come to a huge log and you just know that you and your lion are both going to jump it. One, two, three, jump!

Now your lion is taking longer strides, walking faster and faster… You won't be able to keep this up for long, so you manage to scramble on to its back. That's it! Your lion breaks into a gallop and you hold on for dear life, rocking backwards and forwards… His feet hardly touch the ground and now you feel as if you flying… Yes, you are, you're flying up, up above the trees, over the roofs of the houses and curving back towards the park. What a glorious feeling!

You look down and see your friend sitting all alone on the bench… You wave, and now you are gliding, gliding towards the ground. You land in a soft heap on the ground. Your eyes are closed… Now your best friend is shaking you… Your friend tells you to wake up, because the ankle is better now and it is time to walk on!

Follow-up meditation

Ask the children to sit down, close their eyes and imagine that they are either Adam or Eve... You are standing in a beautiful garden with God. He smiles at you and invites you to walk with him through his garden. As you walk, he seems to match his steps with yours, so that he is always at your side... He points out some beautiful trees with fruit on them. What kind of fruit do they have on them? Now he shows you a tiny bird on a branch. What is it like? Now he beckons and a beautiful horse comes trotting up to make friends with you.

You walk on together, chatting happily. What are you chatting about? Now you are both quiet, but it doesn't matter at all because you feel absolutely at ease... because you know that with a best friend you can be happy whether you are talking or just being quiet together.

Group craft

You will need

A long roll of blank wallpaper divided into five sections to make a 'big picture' mural (see page 73); pencils; crayons; felt-tipped pens; stickers of trees, flowers, stars, animals and footprints

Invite the children to have fun decorating the first section of the 'big picture' mural, headed 'Best friends'. Encourage them to use their imagination to illustrate today's Bible story by drawing Adam and Eve in the garden of Eden, making friends with the animals.

Individual craft

You will need

Rectangles of white paper, about A5 size (one per child); pencils; crayons or felt-tipped pens; sticky tape; scissors

Each piece of paper makes three bracelets, which could be made in advance.

Fold the rectangle of paper in half, short edges together, and then in half again (in the same direction). With the short end of the folded paper towards you, draw a circle (for a face or head shape) near the top of the paper, another circle in the middle and a third near the bottom of the paper. Connect each circle to the long edges of the paper with two lines (rather like a narrow watch strap).

Cut out each bracelet, taking care not to cut along the folds of the 'straps'. Open out the bracelets and invite the children to decorate one each. They could draw their own face on one of the circles and the faces of friends on the others. They might choose to draw the faces of Adam, Eve and two animals from the garden of Eden.

The children could help each other to fasten the bracelets on their wrists with tape. Any children who do not want to wear the bracelets could draw the faces of the group members on the circles and tape the bracelets together to make a chain of friendship.

Prayer

Recap the things you have discovered together. What sort of relationship did God want to have with people? Does he still want this today? Turn back to the list you made, headed 'A best friend is...'. How can we each be a best friend to God? After all, friendship is a two-way thing. Suggestions might include making an effort to get to know God very well; taking an interest in the things God cares about; trying not to let God down; chatting to God regularly; looking after God's world; taking care of each other and so on. One of the ways that we can feel closer to God is to talk to him every day.

Dear God, thank you for creating such an amazing world for us to live in and for giving us everything we need. Please help us to live up to the trust you have placed in us by looking after your world, your plants and animals, and by being good friends to one another. Thank you that you want to be our best friend. Please help us to be your best friends, too, and to walk along at your side this week, this Christmas and all through our lives. Amen

Party bag

Give each child a piece of white card cut in the shape of a mobile phone screen or computer screen. Encourage everyone to keep this card with them over the following week. Each day, they could write God a short message or text, telling him something about their day. One sentence per day would be fine, such as '10Q 4 my friends' ('thank you for my friends'). Perhaps the cards could be brought back the following week to be displayed.

★

Adam and Eve disobey God

> ## Theme
> The broken friendship
>
> ## Bible story
> Genesis 3:1–24

Ready, steady...

Last week's session painted a picture of how God intended the world to be a harmonious place, with human beings in a close relationship with their maker. This week, we see how Adam and Eve separated themselves from God. Even though God put all the resources of the world at their disposal and offered them direct communion with him (through the tree of life in Genesis 2:9), they couldn't resist doing the one thing they had been asked not to do: to eat the fruit that would let them decide for themselves the difference between right and wrong (2:17). God had warned them that this would be a fatal mistake, but they took no notice, egged on by the desire to be as clever as God.

Notice, in Genesis 3, exactly how the crafty snake persuades Eve to eat the forbidden fruit, and what is spoilt as a result (Adam and Eve's friendship with God, their natural relationship with each other, their pleasure in their work, and even their relationship with the natural world). Think how Adam and Eve represent all of us on a daily basis, and the devices we use to persuade ourselves that it is acceptable to give in to a particular temptation. Think about how we manage to resist temptation and about the ways in which people today decide for themselves what is right and wrong, often paying no attention to the consequences.

God banished Adam and Eve from the garden; it was only fair that they should pay the price for going their own way. They were no longer to enjoy eternal life with God but were to be separated from him until they died and returned to dust. But God still loved and provided for them, and, as we now know, God was already planning to rescue his people from their self-imposed predicament.

Go!

Display the friendship bracelet and the Christmas stocking (now with four presents left inside). Start by pointing out that whatever we do or wherever we go, there are usually some rules that we need to know about. Make a list together of different types of rules, such as school rules, rules for crossing the road, road traffic regulations, rules of a sport or board game, the laws of a country, rules laid down by parents and carers, and so on. Do rules spoil our fun? Do they stop us having freedom? When might we be tempted to break a rule?

Icebreaker

You will need

The following five rules of snakes and ladders written on separate postcards; snakes and ladders board game (optional)

1. Each player must throw a six to start.
2. Each player throws the dice and moves the equivalent number of squares along the board.

3. A player landing on the bottom of a ladder can move to the top of that ladder.
4. A player landing on the head of a snake must move to the bottom of that snake.
5. The first player to reach square number 100 is the winner.

Place the five postcards, rule side down, on the floor in no particular order. Ask different children to choose one card each, which they turn over and read to the rest of the group. The group members guess the game and put the rules in the right order as you continue. If you have the board game with you, ask the children to look at the pictures of the snakes and the ladders. Are the rules necessary? What would happen if there were no rules for the game?

Talk about how we might feel if we were playing the game with a friend who cheated and didn't abide by the rules. Would we want to play with this friend again? When might we cheat at a game in order to win? Would we feel as good about winning like this as we would have done if we had followed the rules? How does it feel to let down a good friend or relative in this way?

Dramatised Bible story

Recap the story of how God made Adam and Eve to be his best friends. He gave them everything they needed, and they were happy walking and talking together in the garden of Eden. Explain that today's story is about something dramatic that happened to spoil everything. The stocking contains a clue. Ask someone to pull out the next present and to open it to reveal the toy snake.

Before you read the story together, ask the children to listen carefully in order to discover what rule Adam and Eve were tempted to break, and what was spoiled when they gave in to temptation. The storytelling can be divided among several children.

Narrator 1:	The snake was more cunning than any of the other wild animals that God had made. One day it came to Eve and asked…
Snake:	Did God tell you not to eat fruit from any tree in the garden?
Narrator 1:	Eve answered…
Eve:	God said we could eat fruit from any tree in the garden, except the one in the middle. He told us not to eat fruit from that tree or even to touch it. If we do, we will die.
Narrator 2:	The snake replied…
Snake:	No, you won't! God understands what will happen on the day you eat fruit from that tree. You will see what you have done, and you will know the difference between right and wrong, just as God does.
Narrator 3:	Eve stared at the fruit. It looked beautiful and tasty. She wanted the wisdom that it would give her, and she ate some of the fruit. Adam was there with her, so she gave some to him, and he ate it too.
Narrator 4:	Right away they saw what they had done, and they realised they were naked. Then they sewed fig leaves together to make something to cover themselves.
Narrator 5:	Late in the afternoon a breeze began to blow, and Adam and Eve heard God walking in the garden. They were frightened and hid behind some trees.
Narrator 6:	But the Lord God called out to Adam…

Reproduced with permission from *Seasonal Activities for Christmas Festivities* by Vicki Howie (BRF/Barnabas, 2012)
www.barnabasinchurches.org.uk

God:	Where are you?
Adam:	I was naked, and when I heard you walking through the garden, I was frightened and hid!
God:	How did you know you were naked? Did you eat fruit from that tree in the middle of the garden?
Adam:	It was the woman you put here with me. She gave me some of the fruit, and I ate it.
Narrator 1:	Then God said to Eve…
God:	What have you done?
Narrator 2:	Eve said…
Eve:	The snake tricked me, and I ate some of that fruit.
Narrator 3:	So God said to the snake…
God:	Because of what you have done, for as long as you live you will crawl on your stomach and eat dirt.
Narrator 4:	Then God said to Adam and Eve…
God:	Because you have disobeyed me, you have spoiled my beautiful world. Now you will have to work very hard to produce food from the ground for the rest of your lives. When you grow old, you will die. You were made from the dust and to dust you will return.
Narrator 5:	God made clothes out of animal skins for Adam and Eve to keep them warm.
Narrator 6:	Then God sent them out of the garden of Eden because they had chosen to do what they wanted instead of listening to him.

Reproduced with permission from *Seasonal Activities for Christmas Festivities* by Vicki Howie (BRF/Barnabas, 2012)
www.barnabasinchurches.org.uk

Follow-up discussion

Chat together about the rule that Adam and Eve were tempted to break. What was spoiled when they gave in to temptation? Every day we give in to the temptation to do things that will not please God. Sometimes we lose our tempers, we don't want to share, or we think we know best. Do we feel closer to God when we are doing things that please him or things that make him sad?

Drama games

Traffic lights

Ask everyone to spread out around the room, ready to drive an imaginary vehicle of their choice. Give them a few minutes to decide on their vehicle. (You could ask some children to describe theirs.) Give out the commands below and show everyone how they should respond. Explain that they will need to walk around the room carefully, without bumping into others, and use all the available floor space.

Start by asking everyone to set off, and then use the commands any number of times and in an appropriate order. After a while, eliminate the last children to respond or those who do not respond correctly or sensibly, until you have a winner.

- **Set off**: Switch on the engine and set off
- **Red**: Stand still and silent
- **Amber**: Get ready to go
- **Green**: Start moving
- **Park**: Come to a standstill and switch off the engine
- **Roundabout**: Circle
- **Three-point turn**: Do just that!
- **Reverse**: Go back four steps

Follow-up discussion

Chat about what would happen if we did not have road traffic rules. In what ways are they there for our safety and to allow the traffic to move freely? Which school rules are there for our safety? (For example, not running in the corridors or on the stairs.) Which home rules are there for our safety or our own good? (For example, not touching sharp knives, or not watching television until after homework is finished.) Why do adults make these rules?

Snake alley

> ## You will need
>
> One colourful sock per child (optional)

Choose one child to walk the alley and divide the remaining children into two groups of equal size to form two parallel lines, facing each other (the snake alley). Each child in the two groups could wear a colourful sock on one hand and arm, to represent the snake. Next, read out one of the following five commands.

- Your dad says, 'Don't bounce on the trampoline at the same time as a friend or you might crash heads!'
- Your grandma says, 'Don't buy shoes that might spoil your feet!'
- Your teacher says, 'Don't play too many computer games before bed or you won't be able to get to sleep!'
- Your mum says, 'Don't eat too many sweets before supper or you will spoil your appetite!'
- Your brother says, 'Don't leave all the lights on or it will be a waste of energy!'

Give the children forming the alleyway a short time to think and discuss how they might each persuade the remaining child to disobey the command. Repeat the command.

The snakes respond by saying, 'Did your dad really say don't bounce on the trampoline at the same time as a friend?' As the child walks very slowly down the alleyway, the snakes wave their arms and call out their reasons for disobeying—for example, 'You won't have an accident!'; 'Your dad doesn't want you to have any fun!'; 'Nothing bad will happen!' and so on. At the end of the alleyway, the child must say what he or she has decided to do.

Follow-up discussion

Chat together about times when we think we know best. Point out that our parents and teachers have a lot more experience of life and so it is worth listening to their advice.

How might we help ourselves to be strong and not give in to temptation? Suggestions might include:

- thinking whether we are supposed to do a particular thing
- thinking how good it will feel to stay strong
- remembering how uncomfortable we feel when we do the wrong thing
- remembering that we get stronger every time we make the right decision
- remembering that God is our best friend and we don't want to let him down
- thinking what Jesus would do if he were in the same situation

Group craft

You will need

The wallpaper 'big picture' mural with the second section headed 'The broken friendship'; crayons; felt-tipped pens; stickers

Invite the children to decorate the section with an illustration of today's Bible story. You might like to tell them that artists have often represented the forbidden fruit as an apple.

Individual craft

You will need

Sheets of white paper with a spiral drawn on them, a head at the outside end and a small tail at the centre, to represent a coiled snake (one per child); googly eyes; tongue shapes; thread for hanging

Ask the children to cut out the snake, colour the tongue pink and stick on the eyes and tongue. They should then draw sections on the snake, which can be coloured in either immediately or at home (see the 'Party bag' section below). The thread can be attached to the tail so that the snake hangs in a whirly-twirly fashion.

Follow-up discussion

Chat about the way in which the snake in the story was cunning. Can the children think of things people do today without giving much thought to the consequences? Suggestions might include cutting down rainforests and destroying animal habitats; polluting rivers; polluting the atmosphere by overusing cars and planes; starting wars and so on.

Prayer

Recap the main points of the session, and point out that the things that tempt us often look lovely on the outside but can't really make us happy.

Dear God, we are sorry that we often give in to temptation to do the wrong thing. Sometimes we hurt other people or spoil your beautiful world. Thank you that you keep on loving and caring for us. Please help us to stay strong and to remember that you know what is best for us. Amen

Party bag

Encourage the children to colour in a section of their snake each time they manage to resist a temptation in the coming week.

★

John the Baptist

Theme
Time to say sorry

Bible story
Luke 3:1–22

Ready, steady...

Read the stories about the birth of John the Baptist in Luke 1:5–25 and 57–80, paying particular attention to his father Zechariah's words in verses 67–80. It would be useful to have the story at your fingertips for this week's session.

The stocking present this time is a small mirror and comb set, something we use to 'get ready' most days. John the Baptist was urging people to 'get ready' for Jesus by taking a good look at themselves and turning away from wrong behaviour. He invited them to be baptised in water as an outward sign of their repentance.

Most of us have quarrelled with someone or suffered a broken relationship at some time in our lives. The cause is often our own pride. This week, think about the stages that we need to go through before any reconciliation can take place. It might involve thinking objectively about our own behaviour and trying to judge whether it was hurtful or wrong. This can be a painful process, but it is only when we are brave enough to accept the truth about ourselves that we can feel remorse, apologise with sincerity and resolve to do better in future. It is often difficult to say 'sorry' and mean it. When we hold a mirror up to ourselves, we can sometimes see how our actions might appear to others. With children, this needs to be tackled with a light touch rather than in an accusatory tone.

Go!

Display the friendship bracelet, the toy snake and the Christmas stocking, now with three presents remaining. Chat together about how long it is until Christmas. Ask the children to imagine for a moment that they have never heard of Christmas. What things might they see or hear at home, at school or in the town that would give them a clue that something special is about to happen? Suggestions might include colourful Christmas lights hung up in the town; carols playing on the radio; Christmas cards arriving through the post; packets of mince pies in the supermarket and so on. These are all signs that Christmas is coming.

Icebreaker

You will need

The following sentences written on individual postcards:

- Smoke is billowing from a volcano.
- The petrol sign is lit up on the car dashboard.
- Green shoots are poking up through the soil.
- The head teacher brings a visitor to assembly.
- Your throat is sore and you keep sneezing.
- On the train, your station is announced.

Place the postcards with the sentences face down on the floor. Invite different children to choose a card and read it to the group. Discuss what the different signs may be pointing to and what action might need to be taken in order to be ready for this event.

What actions do we need to take in order to be ready for Christmas? The children may give practical answers such as 'buying Christmas presents'. Be non-committal about their answers at this stage.

Dramatised Bible story

Recap last week's Bible story. Explain that God went on loving people, even though Adam and Eve let him down, and he always helps those who try to please him. You might like to mention some Old Testament characters who are familiar to the children, such as Noah, Joseph and David. Talk about how, all down the ages, people have made God sad by doing the opposite to pleasing him—just like Adam and Eve. However, God's bigger plan is to rescue us from the way we separate ourselves from him by doing what we want instead of what he wants. At the first Christmas, God gave us his Son, Jesus, to show us how to live God's way. Explain that God needed someone to prepare for Jesus' arrival. That person was Jesus' cousin, John the Baptist, who was a little older than Jesus.

Before you read the story together, choose someone to unpack the third present from the stocking and reveal the comb and mirror set. As they listen to the story, ask the children to try to see any connection between this present and John's message. The storytelling can be divided among several children.

Narrator:	John went into the country around the River Jordan. He shouted out…
John:	It's time to get ready for the Lord!
Narrator:	Then he invited the people to show how sorry they were for their bad behaviour by being baptised in the river.
Narrator:	Crowds came to be dipped in the water by him. But some people said…
Voice 1:	Why should we do this?
Voice 2:	God must be pleased with us already because we are the children of Abraham.
Narrator:	But John said…
John:	You can't simply rely on that! You must live lives that please God.
Narrator:	The crowd asked…
Voice 3:	What should we do, then?
Narrator:	John answered…
John:	If you have plenty of food and clothes, you should share them with others who have little.
Narrator:	Some tax collectors came to be baptised and asked him…
Tax collector:	What should we do?
Narrator:	John told them…
John:	Don't take more money from the people than you are supposed to.
Narrator:	Then some soldiers asked him…
Soldier:	And what should we do?
Narrator:	John replied…
John:	Don't tell lies about people, but do your jobs properly.

Reproduced with permission from *Seasonal Activities for Christmas Festivities* by Vicki Howie (BRF/Barnabas, 2012)
www.barnabasinchurches.org.uk

Narrator: As people waited by the river, they wondered if
              John was the special person from God they were
              waiting for. But John told them…

John: I am preparing the way for someone far more
              important than me. I can only baptise you with
              water, but he will shower you with all God's
              blessings. This is the good news that I bring you
              from God.

Follow-up discussion

Discuss the connection between the stocking present and what
John was asking the people to do (the idea of getting ready for
something or someone special). Chat together about the wrong
things the people of the day might have been doing, such as being
greedy and not sharing, cheating and telling lies. Talk about how
John wanted them to get ready for Jesus by living better lives.

Drama games

The mirror game

John wanted people to say sorry, but this can be a hard thing to
do because often we can't see that we have done anything wrong.
Bring out the mirror and suggest that sometimes we need to think
about how our behaviour might appear to others. It is rather like
taking a good look at our actions (not our appearance) in a mirror.

Divide everyone into pairs, facing one another in a kneeling
position. Ask one person from each pair to mime getting ready for
school by washing their face, brushing their teeth, combing their
hair and so on, while the other person copies each mime. Swap over
so that the other person leads the mimes. If you see a particularly
effective pair, ask the others to freeze and watch for a while.

Reproduced with permission from *Seasonal Activities for Christmas Festivities* by Vicki Howie (BRF/Barnabas, 2012)
www.barnabasinchurches.org.uk

End by saying that we can only feel truly sorry for what we have done when we realise how our actions have hurt other people. Then we can mean it when we say sorry.

Turn back!

You will need

A dice and shaker for each team

Divide the children into equal teams and mark a line at one end of the room. Each member of each team must walk to the end of the room by placing one foot directly in front of the other, touching heel to toe, and then walk back again normally. When every member of the team has done this, the team must walk to an object such as a chair and all touch it. The first team 'home' is the winner.

Each team can speed the progress of a team member who is walking heel-to-toe by continually shaking and throwing the dice. As soon as a six is thrown, the team shout, 'Turn back!' and the person then runs back to the finish line. A team member who does not touch heel to toe properly must start again. Any team that does not throw the dice correctly must start the entire game again.

Follow-up discussion

Chat about the meaning of the word 'repent'. John the Baptist asked people not only to be sorry for their bad behaviour, but also to be resolved to turn away from doing wrong in the future. Talk about ways in which we can become more determined to turn away from wrong behaviour, such as thinking about whether our behaviour is unfair or unkind to others, asking ourselves what God would think about it, imagining how it would feel if others did the same thing to us, or asking God for his help not to repeat bad behaviour.

Our speaker today is...

Divide the children into teams. Explain that each team is going to introduce a mystery guest speaker, without saying who they are. Give each team one of the ideas below and allow five minutes for the teams to work out four or five things to say about them.

- A well-known character from a book
- A member of the royal family
- Doctor Who
- Father Christmas
- A well-known Disney character

An example might be as follows.

Child 1:	Our speaker today is someone who works very hard at this time of year.
Child 2:	He is well known for his kindness to children.
Child 3:	He dresses in an unusual way.
Child 4:	He lives in a very cold part of the world.
Child 5:	Our speaker today is...
Everyone:	Father Christmas!

Follow-up discussion

Chat together about why a visiting speaker needs to be introduced. For example, people might need to know who the person is, why they are an expert on their subject, why they might be interesting to listen to, what they have to say that is important and so on. Talk about whether these things apply to John the Baptist introducing Jesus and why it was important for John to show people that they needed Jesus' help to live better lives.

Group craft

You will need

The wallpaper 'big picture' mural unrolled to reveal the section headed 'Time to say sorry'; crayons; felt-tipped pens; stickers

Invite the children to decorate the new section with a picture of John the Baptist speaking to the crowd. Chat together about how John was dressed in a rough camel-skin coat, tied around the waist with a leather belt.

Individual craft

You will need

White card folded into the shape of a greetings card (one per child); crayons; felt-tipped pens; stickers, including some with sad faces

Ask the children to design a 'sorry' card that people might like to buy in a shop and send to someone they have let down or quarrelled with. Encourage them to think about the possible background story before they design the card. What has happened to these two friends? What pictures and words will go on the front and inside of the card? When the cards are ready, you might like to ask different children to explain theirs to the others.

Prayer

Chat together about how God sent John the Baptist to prepare the way for Jesus. Refer to the earlier discussion about how we might get ready for Christmas. How might the ideas have changed during this session? In what ways might God want us to celebrate Jesus' birth that are different from what we have done in the past?

Dear God, thank you for sending John the Baptist to prepare the way for Jesus. We know that sometimes we can't see that we have done anything wrong, and sometimes we say 'sorry' without really meaning it. Please help us to get ready for Christmas by taking a good look at our own behaviour so that we can lead lives that please you. Amen

Party bag

Give everyone a happy face sticker to take home as a reminder that God delights in us and always thinks the best of us. The sticker could be placed on a mirror at home as an encouragement to become the people God wants us to be this Christmas.

★

The prodigal son

Theme
Jesus the go-between

Bible story
Luke 15:11–32

Ready, steady...

This session explores the way Jesus has shown us how much God wants to heal our broken relationship with him. Before Jesus was born, people had long been awaiting the birth of a promised king. They hoped that this new king would lead them to a great victory over the occupying Romans. In fact, Jesus came to do something far more important—to heal our broken relationship with God. In the first stage of this healing process, Jesus came alongside people, befriending them and listening to their stories. For example, Jesus went to the home of Zacchaeus, the dishonest tax collector (see Luke 19:1–10), to share a meal and to talk. As a result of this kindness, Zacchaeus was able to change for the better and make his peace with God.

Jesus told stories, held conversations with people and taught about God in order to explain how we should live and how much God is longing for us to 'turn back' to him. In his parable about the two sons, Jesus likens God to a compassionate father who runs to embrace his repentant son. Jesus could not have achieved all this by shouting instructions from heaven. It was absolutely necessary for him to enter our world, be born as a baby just like us and grow up among us as a friend and brother. Jesus took the role of humility: he put the needs of others first and asks us to do the same.

Think about the healing process in a broken relationship. How do we help to make peace between two people? How do we benefit from a wise go-between? At Christmas, we often find ourselves spending time with people whose lives are very different from our own. For children, it may involve spending time with elderly relations or stepbrothers and sisters. The 'Party bag' activity may help to bring these different 'worlds' a little closer together.

Go!

Display the friendship bracelet, the toy snake, the comb and mirror and the Christmas stocking, which now has just two presents remaining. Recap the 'big picture' so far: God made Adam and Eve to be his best friends; Adam and Eve let God down and spoilt the friendship; God went on loving and caring for people; he sent John the Baptist to prepare the way for Jesus.

Icebreaker

You will need

Five small objects, all to do with repairing or mending—for example, ointment for healing burnt skin; glue for mending broken pots; a needle and thread for mending clothes; a hammer and nails for repairing furniture; a 'sorry' greetings card for mending a friendship

Children might like to play this game in pairs. Give them several minutes to examine all the objects and decide what they are all for.

Next, chat together about the objects and what they might be used to do. Think about what they have in common. Move on to talk about what Jesus was coming to do and how he would mend our broken friendship with God.

Dramatised Bible story

Ask someone to unwrap the present from the stocking to reveal the story CD or book. Chat about stories we can listen to at home or in the car. Point out that Jesus was a great storyteller. He used stories to tell us how God feels about us.

Before you read the story together, ask the children to listen carefully to find out what unkind thing the younger son does in the story, and what happens when the son turns back home. The storytelling can be divided among several children.

Narrator: Jesus told this story…

Jesus: Once a man had two sons. The younger son said to his father…

Son: Give me my share of the family fortune right now!

Jesus: So the father did everything that was necessary and gave the son his share of the family money. Not long after that, the son packed all his belongings and set off for a foreign country. There he wasted the money, buying anything he wanted. After he had spent everything, there was a severe famine in that country. There was no food to eat and the son was very hungry. So he went to get a job on a local farm.

Son: Please, can you give me a job on your farm?

Farmer: Yes, all right. You can go into the fields and feed my pigs.

Reproduced with permission from *Seasonal Activities for Christmas Festivities* by Vicki Howie (BRF/Barnabas, 2012)
www.barnabasinchurches.org.uk

Jesus:	The son was so hungry, he would have been glad to eat what the pigs were eating, but no one gave him a thing. Finally, he came to his senses and said...
Son:	Even my father's workers have plenty to eat, and here I am, starving to death. I will go back to my father and say to him, 'Father, I have behaved so badly towards you and towards God. I don't deserve to be treated like your son any more. But please give me a job on the family farm.'
Jesus:	The younger son set off for home. But while he was still a long way off, his father saw him and felt sorry for him. He ran to his son, threw his arms around him and kissed him. The son said to him...
Son:	Father, I have sinned against God and against you. I am no longer good enough to be called your son.
Jesus:	But the father said to his servants...
Father:	Quick! Bring the best clothes for him. Give him a ring for his finger and sandals for his feet. Bring the best calf and prepare it. Let's celebrate! For this son of mine was as good as dead and now I have him home again; he was lost and now he is found.
Jesus:	So they began to celebrate.
Narrator:	There is great rejoicing in heaven whenever someone turns back towards God.

Follow-up discussion

Talk about the unkind thing the younger son did in the story by demanding that his father give him his share of the family money and leaving home. It was almost as if he wished his father was dead.

Reproduced with permission from *Seasonal Activities for Christmas Festivities* by Vicki Howie (BRF/Barnabas, 2012)
www.barnabasinchurches.org.uk

He didn't care at all about his father's feelings. He didn't care that his father needed help to run the farm. He let his father down.

Chat about what happened when the son turned back home. He was hoping that his father would give him a job on the farm, but his father did far more than this. Talk about how the father ran out to meet his son and gave him a hug. He dressed him in fine clothes and then he threw a party to celebrate his return. He was so happy that his son had come to his senses. Think about who the father represents in this story and why Jesus told the story. Jesus wants his friends and followers to 'turn back' to God, like the son in the story.

Drama games

Let's be friends again!

Ask the children to sit in threes, with a little space between groups. Remind them that Jesus came to make peace again between us and God. It could be said that he acted as a go-between.

Ask each group to appoint a go-between, and explain that the other two are 'friends'. The friends need to talk in a friendly manner towards each other until you call out, 'Freeze'. They then allow their conversation to develop into a realistic argument. At the second 'Freeze', ask the go-between to try to make peace between the two friends by listening to each side and suggesting a sensible compromise. Play the game again, allowing different people to be the peacemakers.

Topics for 'argument' might include whose turn it is to watch a favourite television programme and whose fault it is that a favourite toy is broken. If appropriate, one of the groups might like to do an action replay for everyone to watch.

Follow-up discussion

Chat about someone who helped to settle an argument. How easy is it to make peace between two friends? What might be involved? You might like to mention international peacemakers who try to solve differences between countries.

Step into the frame!

Divide the children into small groups. Each group needs to appoint someone to take the role of a photographer from the local paper who has come to capture one of the scenes suggested below. Allow a minute or two for the 'photographers' to arrange their subjects in suitable poses. At 'Say cheese and freeze!' the photographers pretend to take the shot. Scenes could include a fashion show, a circus scene, a sports team, a wedding and so on.

Next, explain that the photographers are going to set their cameras to automatic. At the words 'Step into the frame!' the photographers must quickly place themselves in the picture as everyone calls out, 'Five, four, three two, one... smile!' The groups then appoint a different photographer and the game continues with another scene.

Follow-up discussion

Chat about possible links between the Christmas story and the game everyone has just played. For example, God entered his own creation, his own world, by giving us Jesus to be born as a baby and to grow up among us. Talk about how, because Jesus was there in person, he was able to make friends with people and tell them stories, such as the one read earlier, which showed how much God loves us.

Group craft

Invite the children to have fun designing a picture that symbolises Jesus' role as peacemaker between God and us. This might be a picture of Jesus telling a story to a crowd of people, or it could be a more symbolic diagram showing the word 'Jesus' linking the words 'God' and 'us'.

Individual craft

Explain that the dove is often used as a symbol of peace. Help the children to cut slits for the wings and tail. Fold each piece of paper backwards and forwards lengthways as if you were making a fan. Thread one piece through the slit for the wings and the other through the slit for the tail. Fold them upwards and secure with some sticky tape. Draw eyes on the face and stick on a loop of ribbon for hanging the dove.

Talk about how the action of folding the paper backwards and forwards is like Jesus going between us and God: we give him our prayers and he brings us God's love.

Prayer

Chat about how, after an argument, we sometimes feel afraid to say sorry in case the other person still feels cross with us. Jesus tells us that God is ready and waiting to make friends with us again, just like the father in our story.

Dear Jesus, we are sorry that we often let God down by thinking only about ourselves. Thank you that you show us how to live, and how much God wants to be good friends with us. Please help us to remember to say 'sorry' to God when we let him down and to know that he will always forgive us. Thank you for all those who work to bring peace. Please help us to be peacemakers among our friends and in our families this Christmas. Amen

Party bag

Give each child a circle of white card shaped like a large Christmas tree bauble, divided into sections with pencil lines. Suggest that they fill the sections with drawings of people and things that are important to them, such as a good friend, a computer, a church, a pet, a football, a musical instrument and so on. The baubles could be coloured, decorated with glitter and hung on the Christmas tree with ribbon. Encourage everyone to use their bauble as a talking point with relatives over the Christmas period. Other members of the family might like to make their own Christmas baubles to promote family interaction.

★

Jesus' crucifixion and resurrection

> **Theme**
> For ever friends
>
> **Bible story**
> Luke 23:32–46

Ready, steady...

Re-read John 1:1–18, which summarises the Bible story from creation to the birth of John the Baptist. In this passage, Jesus is described as the human expression of the loving purpose of God to create life, care for it and bring it into the right relationship with him. In verse 17, John explains that while the law was given through Moses, Jesus brought us undeserved kindness and truth. Dying for us, he reconciled us to God and gave us the gift of eternal life.

The icebreaker game aims to demonstrate that our everyday actions have consequences not only for others but also for ourselves. The Bible story goes on to show that Jesus has paid the price for our disobedience in going our own way and flouting God's authority. Jesus fought a great battle with sin on the cross in order to bring us forgiveness, freedom from the consequences of our sins, and friendship with God.

Allow plenty of time for the drama game on this theme to encourage quiet concentration. This week we will be thinking about what it means to show grace towards others—something we often need in abundance at Christmas time.

Go!

Display the Christmas stocking, now with just one present left inside. Recap the discussion about different rules that we often need to follow (see page 87). What happens when we break these rules?

Icebreaker

You will need

Twelve small pieces of paper, each with one of the following broken rules or related penalties written on them and placed around the room

- Overdue library book / 50p fine
- Talking in class / detention
- Football foul / penalty given to other team
- Speeding / penalty points on driving licence
- Crossing the road without looking / serious injury
- Not drinking enough water / headache

Point out that when we break a rule or do something silly, there is usually a price to pay. For example, if we eat too much chocolate or drink too many fizzy drinks, the price we pay is feeling unwell.

Explain that there are six actions and their matching penalties placed around the room. Ask the children to wander around, simply reading them. Then, at the call 'Pay the price!' everyone should sort the pieces of paper into matching pairs.

Follow-up discussion

Chat about how Adam and Eve ate fruit from the tree that gave the power to decide the difference between right and wrong, even though God had told them not to. God had warned them that the result would be very serious and they would eventually die. Talk about how we are just like Adam and Eve, because we often do things that we know we shouldn't. We try to tell ourselves that it doesn't really matter. However, God loves us so much that he gave us Jesus to save us from paying the price for the way we behave. How did he do this? Perhaps the last present in the stocking will give us a clue.

Dramatised Bible story

Ask someone to pull out the last present and open it, revealing the jewellery cross. Talk about how Jesus died on the cross to open up the way to heaven for us, so that one day we can live with God for ever. We can now be friends for ever with God, just as he had intended right back in the beginning.

Before you read the story together, ask the children to listen carefully to find out what Jesus had done wrong, and where Jesus said one of the criminals would be later that day. The storytelling can be divided among several children.

Narrator 1: Two criminals were led out with Jesus to be killed.

Narrator 2: When the soldiers came to the hill called 'The Skull', they nailed him to a wooden cross. The two criminals were also nailed to crosses, one on his right and the other on his left. Jesus said…

Reproduced with permission from *Seasonal Activities for Christmas Festivities* by Vicki Howie (BRF/Barnabas, 2012)
www.barnabasinchurches.org.uk

Jesus:	Father, forgive them, for they don't understand what they are doing.
Narrator 3:	The soldiers divided up his clothes between them.
Narrator 4:	The people stood watching and the Jewish leaders made fun of him. They said…
Leader 1:	You saved others! Let's see if you can save yourself…
Leader 2:	… if you are God's special one!
Narrator 1:	One of the criminals who hung there on the next cross said…
Criminal 1:	So you're the Messiah, are you? Well then, why don't you save us all?
Narrator 2:	But the other criminal told him to be quiet. He said…
Criminal 2:	We deserve to die for the things we have done. But Jesus has done nothing wrong.
Narrator 3:	Then he said…
Criminal 2:	Jesus, please remember me when you become the ruler of your kingdom.
Narrator 4:	Jesus answered him…
Jesus:	The truth is that you will be with me in heaven this very day.
Narrator 1:	At midday the sun stopped shining, and darkness came over the whole land until three in the afternoon.
Narrator 2:	And the curtain of the temple was torn in two.
Narrator 3:	Then Jesus called out in a loud voice…
Jesus:	Father, I put myself in your hands.
Narrator 4:	When he had said this, he died.

Reproduced with permission from *Seasonal Activities for Christmas Festivities* by Vicki Howie (BRF/Barnabas, 2012)
www.barnabasinchurches.org.uk

Follow-up discussion

Chat about the fact that Jesus had done nothing wrong, and yet he paid the ultimate price when he died on the cross so that he could open the door to heaven for us all. Jesus told one of the criminals that he would be with Jesus in heaven. This criminal was sorry for what he had done and he believed in Jesus.

Drama game

Put the children into groups of three. Ask two children in each group to stand in a relaxed manner, and explain that they are the 'clay'. The third child is the 'sculptor' and moulds them into a sculpture entitled 'For ever friends'. The game is played in complete silence. The sculptors demonstrate the facial expressions they require on their own faces. Allow plenty of time, as the sculptors may wish to start again if they are not happy with the results.

Ask the sculptors to look at all the completed works of art. What story does each one tell? Are there any similarities between any of them? Allow the groups to swap roles and to model 'forgiveness' and then 'freedom'. Finally, talk about how Jesus died on the cross to win us forgiveness for the wrong things we do, freedom from the penalty that we deserve and friendship with God for ever.

Group craft

You will need

The wallpaper 'big picture' mural, open at the fifth and last section, headed 'For ever friends'; crayons; felt-tipped pens; pencils; stickers

Invite the children to decorate the section with a picture of the three crosses on the hillside. A silhouette drawing might be dramatic: colour the sky black but leave the hill and crosses white.

Individual craft

You will need

Pieces of white card cut into the shape of a door sign (one per child); crayons; felt-tipped pens; decorating materials such as glitter or stickers

Chat together about how Jesus rose from the dead on Easter Sunday. He met and talked with some of his friends to show them that he was alive. Explain that after this, Jesus went back to heaven in order to make a place ready for us there. He said, 'There are many rooms in my Father's house' (John 14:2). Invite the children to have fun decorating a room sign with their own name (as per the sample opposite) and to hang it on their bedroom door.

Prayer

Chat together about why Christmas is important—because it celebrates the birth of Jesus, who brought us back into friendship with God. Talk about how Jesus died on the cross for us, even though he had done nothing wrong. In doing this, he brought us friendship with God for ever.

Dear God, thank you for giving us your Son, Jesus, the Saviour of the world. He died on the cross for us even though he had done nothing wrong, and he opened the door to heaven for each one of us. Please

help us to remember what Jesus did for us when we are celebrating Christmas. Help us to be kind to our families and friends this Christmas. Amen

Party bag

Give everyone a small rectangle of white card divided up into squares and with the shape of a cross outlined in coloured ink. Encourage them to complete the cross over the Christmas holidays by colouring in a square every time they manage to keep smiling in a difficult situation. Explain that often what feels like a defeat is, in fact, a victory.

Christmas unpacked

> ### You will need
>
> The Christmas stocking filled with the five unwrapped presents; the wallpaper mural (optional)

Narrator 1:	We've been finding out...
All:	Why Christmas is so important!
Narrator 2:	Each week, we opened a present from a Christmas stocking.

Hold up the filled stocking.

Narrator 3:	Each present led us to a different Bible story.
Narrator 4:	When we had explored all five stories, we saw how they all hang together to make one big story...
All:	The story of our friendship with God.
Narrator 5:	And we saw how the Christmas story fits in.

Pause.

Narrator 1:	We opened the first present to find...
All:	A friendship bracelet!

Reproduced with permission from *Seasonal Activities for Christmas Festivities* by Vicki Howie (BRF/Barnabas, 2012)
www.barnabasinchurches.org.uk

Narrator 2: We read the story about God making Adam and Eve, and we saw that God wanted to be good friends with them.

Child 1: He made them a beautiful home.

Child 2: He gave them plenty of food.

Child 3: He trusted them with his lovely world.

Child 4: He walked and talked with them.

All: They were the best of friends.

Narrator 3: He even tried to protect them by warning them not to eat the fruit from a harmful tree. God said...

God: You may eat fruit from any tree in the garden, except the one that has the power to let you decide the difference between right and wrong. If you eat fruit from that tree, you will die.

Narrator 4: God loved Adam and Eve and he knew what was best for them.

Narrator 5: We all thought about how we could be good friends with God today...

Child 1: By making an effort to get to know him.

Child 2: Looking after his world.

Child 3: Trying not to let him down.

Child 4: Keeping in touch with him every day with just a short prayer...

All: Just like a text message!

Pause.

Narrator 1: We opened the next present, and out slithered...

Reproduced with permission from *Seasonal Activities for Christmas Festivities* by Vicki Howie (BRF/Barnabas, 2012)
 www.barnabasinchurches.org.uk

All:	A slippery snake! Hiss!
Narrator 2:	Not just any snake, but a very crafty one.
Narrator 3:	The snake told Eve that it wouldn't really matter if she ate the forbidden fruit. It said…
Snake:	Die? You won't die! No, it's just that God doesn't want you to be as clever as him!
Narrator 4:	Well, the fruit looked good, and Adam and Eve liked the idea of being as clever as God. And so they ate the fruit.
All:	Oh, no!
Narrator 5:	What a way to treat their best friend! No wonder God sent them out of his garden!
All:	One broken friendship!
Narrator 1:	We realised that we are just like Adam and Eve when we ignore God's friendly voice and proudly go our own way.
Narrator 2:	But God loves his children and he had a rescue plan up his sleeve.
Narrator 3:	He planned to give us his own Son, Jesus, to show us how to live.

Pause.

Narrator 4:	Next, we opened the third present, and found…
All:	A little mirror and comb.
Narrator 5:	Just right for getting ready for a Christmas party!
Narrator 1:	It led us to the story of John the Baptist, because it was his job to get the people ready to meet Jesus. He shouted out…

Reproduced with permission from *Seasonal Activities for Christmas Festivities* by Vicki Howie (BRF/Barnabas, 2012)
www.barnabasinchurches.org.uk

John:	It's time to get ready for Jesus! Start new lives that please God!
All:	It's time to say sorry!
Narrator 2:	It was just as if he was holding up a mirror to the people so that they could see what they were doing wrong.
Narrator 3:	We thought about the things that we do to get ready for Christmas…
Child 1:	Shopping.
Child 2:	Partying.
Child 3:	Making our Christmas lists.
Narrator 4:	And we wondered if this would really please God.
Narrator 5:	So instead, we thought about the things that would really make God happy.
Child 1:	Being kind to others.
Child 2:	Thinking about our actions.
Child 3:	Being truly sorry when we hurt others.
Child 4:	And not doing it again!

Pause.

Narrator 1:	At last, Jesus was born. He came into the world to mend our broken friendship with God. But how would he do this?
Narrator 2:	We opened the fourth present, to find…
All:	A story CD! [*or* A story book!]
Narrator 3:	It led us to a wonderful story that Jesus told— the story of the son who ran away from his loving father.

Narrator 4:   When the son came to his senses, he turned back towards home. But when he was still a long way off, his father came running out to give him a hug. His father said…

Father: Let's celebrate! For this son of mine was as good as dead and now I have him home again. He was lost and now he is found.

Narrator 5:   Jesus told this story to show us that God is loving and forgiving. He longs to make friends with us again.

Narrator 1:   Jesus wanted to make peace between us and God.

All: Jesus the go-between!

Narrator 2:   So we thought about being peacemakers this Christmas…

Narrator 3:   By making an effort to step into each other's worlds.

Pause.

Narrator 4:   When we opened the fifth present in the stocking, we found…

All: A cross!

Narrator 5:   This led us to the Easter story, where Jesus died on the cross for us.

Narrator 1:   He paid the price for us, even though he hadn't done anything wrong.

Narrator 2:   And he opened up the way for us to be friends with God.

All: For ever friends!

Pause.

Narrator 3:   So now we can see the big picture…

Hold up wallpaper mural.

Narrator 4:   At Christmas, we celebrate the birth of Jesus our Saviour…

Narrator 5:   Who died on the cross for us…

Hold up cross, then replace it in the stocking.

Narrator 1:   And told us wonderful stories…

Hold up the story CD or book and then replace it in the stocking.

Narrator 2:   … that reflect God's love for us.

Hold up the mirror and comb, then replace them in the stocking.

Narrator 3:   He defeated our disobedience…

Hold up the snake and then replace it in the stocking.

Narrator 4:   And made us friends with God again.

Hold up the friendship bracelet and then replace it in the stocking.

All: Happy Christmas, everyone!

The gift of Christmas

Themes

Homeless people; lonely people; every nation; refugees; each one of us

Introduction

In this programme, five Christmas stories lead us to think about the people Jesus came to befriend and those whom God wants us to remember at Christmas time. The stories are as follows.

- No room at the inn (homeless people)
- The shepherds (lonely people)
- The wise men (every nation)
- The flight into Egypt (refugees)
- The presentation in the temple (each one of us)

Through a variety of games, discussions, crafts and prayer, we are encouraged to think about how it feels to be homeless, lonely or a refugee. We examine what it means to have respect for different cultures and to see all people as one big human family. In the final session, we think about how Jesus was born as a baby because he came to be a personal friend and Saviour to each one of us.

For this programme, you will need a small Christmas tree or some bare branches in a vase, on which you can hang five tree decorations, simply made from traditional luggage labels or gift tags (available at most post offices or stationery shops). The instructions for these decorations are included in the craft section for each session, and the children make their own to take home. Each decoration symbolises one of the five groups of people, as follows:

- The stable (homeless people)
- A shepherd (lonely people)
- A wise man (every nation)
- A donkey (refugees)
- Baby Jesus (each one of us)

You may like to visit a craft store so that you can buy the materials for all the tree decorations in advance. Before the first session, obtain an overview by reading through all the material in the programme, including the presentation on pages 177–181, which acts as a summary. Ideally, encourage any helpers to do the same so that you are all working towards the same goal.

You will need a nativity stable and a set of nativity figures if the children are going to create a nativity scene week by week.

If you are planning to perform the presentation, you might like to start making any practical arrangements for this now.

★

No room at the inn

> ## Theme
> Homeless people
>
> ## Bible story
> Luke 2:1–7

Ready, steady...

This first session explores the circumstances that left Jesus homeless at his birth and how the good news of Christmas is for all people, including those who are homeless. Some scholars think that the census that took Mary and Joseph to Bethlehem was not for taxation purposes but to show allegiance to Caesar Augustus. (A census of this sort took place in 5BC, about a year before the death of Herod.) Either way, the couple, far from home, were given shelter by someone who was moved by their desperate situation. The stable is used as a symbol of those who are homeless.

If possible, look at the websites of charities for homeless people, such as St Mungo's (www.mungos.org). Read the real-life stories of people who have experienced homelessness, noting how they came to be in this situation. Discover what the charities can offer them. Our homes are important to us and, while there is much that we may appreciate about them, equally we need to deal sensitively with any situation in which a home may not be a place of safety for a particular child.

Go!

Display the bare branches or small tree as you chat together about why we give presents at Christmas. Talk about how God gave us the gift of his Son, Jesus, at the first Christmas. Jesus' birth was very good news because he had come to be our friend and to show us how to live in a way that pleases God.

Jesus was God's present, but who exactly was this present for? Explain that over the next five weeks, you'll be finding the answer to this question and hanging a different decoration on the tree each week as a symbol of a particular group of people. Perhaps the icebreaker game will give us a clue as to the first group.

Icebreaker

You will need

Twelve pieces of paper, each with one of the following animals or homes written on it, and placed around the room: bird, nest, badger, sett, horse, stable, beaver, dam, sheep, fold, fox, den

Talk about favourite animals and explain that you have placed the names of six animals and their homes on pieces of paper around the room. At the call, 'Home sweet home!' the children collect up the pieces of paper and match each animal with its correct home.

Write the following mixed-up Bible verse on a large piece of paper.

Luke doesn't own birds and the nests have to have dens of a Man but have his Foxes call place (Son 9:58).

When the children have matched the animals and homes, see if they can sort out the Bible verse. (See the correct version in the prayer section on page 137.)

Discuss what we look forward to about going home, such as exchanging news with our families; having a meal; being able to relax; having a safe place for our special things; keeping clean and healthy; shelter and warmth.

Think about people who don't have a home—those who are homeless and have to sleep on a pavement or park bench. Which of the above things can they look forward to? Which things would not be available to them?

Dramatised Bible story

Before you read the Bible story together, ask the children to listen carefully to find out who was homeless and why this was so. The storytelling can be divided among several children.

Narrator 1:   About that time, the Emperor Augustus gave orders for the names of all the people to be listed in record books.

Narrator 2:   Everyone had to go to their own home town to be listed. So Joseph had to leave Nazareth in Galilee and go to Bethlehem in Judea.

Narrator 3:   Long ago, Bethlehem had been King David's home town, and Joseph went there because he was from David's family.

Narrator 4:   Mary was engaged to Joseph and travelled with him to Bethlehem.

Narrator 5:   She was soon going to have a baby, and while they were there she gave birth to her firstborn son.

Reproduced with permission from *Seasonal Activities for Christmas Festivities* by Vicki Howie (BRF/Barnabas, 2012)
www.barnabasinchurches.org.uk

Narrator 1:   She dressed him in baby clothes and laid him
               in a bed of hay, because there was no room for
               them in the inn.

Follow-up discussion

Chat about who was homeless. Mary and Joseph couldn't find
anywhere to stay in Bethlehem, so Jesus was born in a borrowed
stable and laid in a borrowed manger.

Talk about why Mary and Joseph had travelled to Bethlehem and
explain that, because of the census, they had to register their names
in the town that Joseph's family came from.

The gift of Christmas
nativity scene

You will need

A nativity stable; a set of nativity figures

Choose some children to bring out the stable and place the figures
of Mary, Joseph and Jesus in the manger inside. Talk about how
uncomfortable the stable would have been. Discuss the dirt,
draughts, rough straw, smells and noise of any animals there.

Reproduced with permission from *Seasonal Activities for Christmas Festivities* by Vicki Howie (BRF/Barnabas, 2012)
www.barnabasinchurches.org.uk
133

Drama games

Sleeping rough

You will need

For the street scene: sleeping bags; newspapers; old blankets; cardboard boxes; a selection of old hats, scarves and gloves
For the soup kitchen: a bright tablecloth; paper napkins; paper plates; plain biscuits; writing icing; a simple snack such as packet soup to mix; bread rolls; cooked sausages

Divide the children into two teams. Ask the first team to dress up in the old clothes and make a street scene using the available materials, as if on a freezing December night. Ask them to step into role and to act and speak as if they really are homeless.

While they are doing this, the other team sets a table and lays out a simple snack for the homeless people, which they serve to them as soon as it is ready.

The teams then swap over and make a new street scene and snack.

Finally, talk about the work of charities for homeless people: going out to find people who are sleeping on the streets; taking them to an emergency shelter where they may be given warm clothes, hot food, a bath, medicine and so on. Sometimes a vet will even check a homeless person's dog. Some charities give training to homeless people—for example, in computer skills, so that they can get a job, start to earn some money and eventually rent a small flat.

Musical homes

You will need

Chairs or cushions to represent 'homes' (one less than the number of children playing); music CD; CD player

Play this game to emphasise a feeling of loss when the chair or cushion 'home' has been taken away.

Place the 'homes' back to back in two lines. When the music starts, everyone walks around them. When the music stops, everyone tries to sit on a home. The one who doesn't get to a home is out. A home is taken away and the game continues. The last child left in is the winner.

Fox and rabbits

You will need

At least four players—a 'fox' and several 'rabbits'

Play this game to emphasise the safety of home.

The fox has a den at one end of the room and the others (the rabbits) have a burrow (or home base) as far away as possible from the den. The rabbits bunny-hop about the room, pretending to look for food and chanting, 'Fox, fox, come out of your den. Whoever you catch can be one of your men.'

The fox then chases the rabbits, who bunny-hop to their burrow for safety. If the fox touches anyone three times before they get back home, the fox takes that rabbit back to the den and they become a fox too.

Craft activities

Gift tag decoration

You will need

Traditional luggage labels or gift tags (one per child); parcel ribbon; a selection of pictures cut from old magazines showing materials suitable for the stable exterior, such as wood, stone, natural carpets, basketwork, tiling, beams, doors and so on; strips of raffia; star sweets in silver foil; scissors; glue; sticky tape

Show the children a decoration that you have made earlier (see example below). Hang the tag on the branches or tree and talk about how Jesus was homeless when he was born, and how the gift of

Christmas is for all people, including those who are homeless. Jesus wants us to remember homeless people at Christmas.

To make the decoration, tie parcel ribbon through the hole in the tag for hanging. Cut and glue small pieces of magazine paper to the lower part of the tag to make the stable wall or doors. Glue strips of raffia to the top part for the roof. Finally, tape the star sweet to the roof.

Prayer

Give the correct version of the muddled Bible verse:

Foxes have dens, and birds have nests, but the Son of Man doesn't have a place to call his own (Luke 9:58).

Chat about how Jesus grew up in Nazareth, where Joseph taught him to be a carpenter. When Jesus was 30 years old, he left home to start God's work, walking from village to village and telling people about God. He often did not know exactly where he would spend the next night. Anyone who wanted to follow him had to be ready to live the same life. Talk about whether Jesus would understand what it is like to be homeless.

Dear God, thank you for the shelter, warmth, laughter and friendliness of our homes. We are sorry that we often take our families, food and clothing for granted and forget to say 'thank you'. We pray for all those who are without homes this Christmas and for those who will give up the comfort of their own homes to go out and help them. Amen

Party bag

Give everyone some white card cut into the shape of a house, with the outline of a door and five windows drawn on it. Invite the children to draw someone or something they are grateful for at home, each day, inside one of the outlines. The pictures might include a plate of biscuits, a bed, a shower, a pet dog or a brother or sister. The children could write 'Home Sweet Home' across the roof, punch holes in the shape and hang it up with ribbon, to help them focus on their homes in the coming week. Decorated, it could even be given as a Christmas present to someone who looks after them at home.

The shepherds

Theme
Lonely people

Bible story
Luke 2:8–20

Ready, steady...

This session explores the story of the shepherds and shows that the good news of Christmas is for all people, including those who live on the fringes of society. Shepherds must have lived a lonely life on the edge of a village or town, watching over the sheep as they grazed on grass or on the stubble left after the harvest. In the summer, when the grass had dried up in the hot sun, the shepherd had to lead his flock further away in order to find green pasture. In fact, he spent so much time alone with the sheep that he learned to know them all by name and could identify which families they belonged to. In this session, the shepherd is used as a symbol of all those who lead a lonely life or feel rejected or ignored.

Jesus himself experienced rejection, beginning with his hostile reception in Nazareth at the start of his ministry (Luke 4:14–30), through to his betrayal by Judas (22:1–6), abandonment by Peter (22:54–62) and, eventually, death on the cross. During his ministry, he made a point of befriending those who had been rejected by society—for example, a man with leprosy (Luke 5:12–14), a blind beggar (18:35–43) and Zacchaeus the tax collector (19:1–10).

Think about people who live on the fringes of society today and identify the possible reasons for this. For example, an elderly person might feel left out because of problems with hearing, sight, mobility or understanding modern technology. Again, a child carer who is responsible for household jobs might have little time to relax with friends after school.

Go!

Display the small Christmas tree or bare branches, with the stable tree decoration hung on it from last week as a reminder of homeless people. Who else can we remember at Christmas time? Perhaps the icebreaker will give us a clue.

Icebreaker

You will need

About six items placed around the room that might be thrown out by a household or could be found in the rubbish, such as vegetable peelings, an odd sock, stale bread, an empty cereal box, an old newspaper and a broken toy

Ask the children to form pairs. Allow them time to examine each of the objects, and then ask different pairs to describe one of them. What do all the objects have in common? (They are all things that might be thrown out.) Explain that there are some people today who feel as if they have been 'thrown out' by everyone else. People might feel like this because they are homeless, elderly or living on their own, or perhaps because they have disabilities, work shifts at night or care for others.

Discuss the reasons why some people might find it difficult to join in with things that are going on. Point out that God loves and values everyone. No one is rubbish to him.

Dramatised Bible story

The Bible story today is about some people who lived a very lonely life. On the night when Jesus was born, there were shepherds looking after their sheep in the fields outside Bethlehem. They worked outside the town and they watched over their sheep day and night. But one night, God included them in something amazing.

Before you read the story together, ask the children to listen carefully to find out who the angel says the good news is for, and why the shepherds were drawn into Bethlehem. The storytelling can be divided among several children.

Narrator 1:   That night, in the fields near Bethlehem, some shepherds were guarding their sheep.

Narrator 2:   All at once an angel came down to them from the Lord, and the brightness of the Lord's glory flashed around them.

Narrator 3:   The shepherds were frightened, but the angel said…

Angel: Don't be afraid! I have good news for you, which will make everyone happy. This very day in King David's home town a Saviour was born for you. He is Christ the Lord. You will know who he is, because you will find him dressed in baby clothes and lying on a bed of hay.

Narrator 3:   Suddenly many other angels came down from heaven and joined in praising God. They said…

Reproduced with permission from *Seasonal Activities for Christmas Festivities* by Vicki Howie (BRF/Barnabas, 2012)
www.barnabasinchurches.org.uk

All:	Praise God in heaven! Peace on earth to everyone who pleases God.
Narrator 1:	After the angels had left and gone back to heaven, the shepherds said to each other...
Shepherd 1:	Let's go to Bethlehem and see what the Lord has told us about.
Narrator 2:	They hurried off and found Mary and Joseph, and they saw the baby lying on a bed of hay.
Narrator 3:	When the shepherds saw Jesus, they told his parents what the angel had said about him.
Narrator 1:	Everyone listened and was surprised, but Mary kept thinking about all this and wondering what it meant.
Narrator 2:	As the shepherds returned to their sheep, they were praising God and saying wonderful things about him.
Narrator 3:	Everything they had seen and heard was just as the angel had said.

Follow-up discussion

Chat together about the angel's message that the good news is for everyone, and about the shepherds hurrying into Bethlehem to see Jesus. The angels announced his birth to humble shepherds living on the fringes of the town.

Reproduced with permission from *Seasonal Activities for Christmas Festivities* by Vicki Howie (BRF/Barnabas, 2012)
www.barnabasinchurches.org.uk

The gift of Christmas nativity scene

You will need

A nativity stable; a set of nativity figures

Choose some children to place the shepherds in the stable, alongside Mary, Joseph and baby Jesus in the manger. Jesus has come to be a friend to those who are lonely and sometimes feel left out.

Drama games

Disco dancing

You will need

CD of popular music; CD player; a flashing disco lantern (optional)

Ask for two volunteers to dance to the music (they could be two leaders). After a while, call out, 'Join the dance!' The two dancers choose two new people to join in. Continue in this way so that more and more children are dancing, until you eventually call 'All join in!' so that no one is left out. Play the game again with two new volunteers and a different track.

Follow-up discussion

Chat about whether the children enjoyed watching or taking part the most. If we don't feel we are good at joining in with things, what might help us to participate more? Discuss the importance of encouraging or inviting others to join in a game or activity so that they do not feel left out.

It feels like...

> ### You will need
>
> Some everyday objects; a basket or box; a small tablecloth or similar

Place the objects in the basket or box and cover the top with the tablecloth. Invite different children to identify the objects just by feeling them. You might like to make this into a team game, using identical objects for each team and scoring a point for a correct answer.

Follow-up discussion

Chat about things that people with visual problems would find difficult to do. How might it affect their lives? You could talk about the value of Braille and guide dogs, both of which help visually impaired people to take part in life more fully. You could suggest that, one day, somebody in the group might invent something that would make the lives of people with disabilities much easier.

Getting to know you...

Ask an older member of your congregation, who has an interesting or exciting story to tell, to come and speak to the children for a few minutes. Invite the children to ask questions.

Individual craft

> ## You will need
>
> Traditional luggage labels or gift tags (one per child); string or twine; stripy or patterned paper; plain coloured paper; white paper; small striped candy canes; glue; sticky tape; scissors

Show the children a completed shepherd tree decoration (see example below). Hang it on the small tree or bare branches to show that the gift of Christmas is for those who live lonely lives.

To make the decoration, tie string or twine through the hole in the tag for hanging. Cut the shepherd's headdress from the stripy or patterned paper, in the same shape as the top half of the tag (the end with the punched hole). Cut the skirt shape from the plain coloured paper, to more than cover the bottom half of the tag. Glue on the skirt and then the headdress. Cut a small circle of white paper, draw a face on it and glue it to the headdress. Glue a short length of twine around the head. Finally stick on the candy cane.

Prayer

Chat about why we look forward to spending Christmas with our families. What might it feel like to spend Christmas Day all alone? Point out that it is often difficult for people who are alone at Christmas while others are having fun with relatives and friends.

Dear God, when we feel lonely or left out, help us to remember that Jesus is our friend. When we feel like rubbish, help us to remember how valuable we are to you. Please help us to show friendship to anyone who is feeling lonely or left out this Christmas. Amen

Party bag

Suggest that, with the help of their parents, the children could make a small stocking (perhaps using a pretty sock) for an elderly or lonely neighbour. This could be filled with small items such as a satsuma, some sweets, a small packet of tea, some wrapped mince pies, a Christmas card, a small pack of biscuits, some Christmas paper napkins and so on.

★

The wise men

> ### Theme
> Every nation
>
> ### Bible story
> Matthew 2:1–12

Ready, steady...

In this session, the wise men who travelled to Bethlehem from a far country are used as a symbol of people from every nation. During his ministry, Jesus often showed that he had come for all people. In John 10:1–21, he refers to himself as the good shepherd and says, 'I have other sheep that are not in this sheep pen. I must bring them together too, when they hear my voice. Then there will be one flock of sheep and one shepherd' (v. 16). In Luke 7:1–10, Jesus helps a centurion, a citizen of an occupying power, by healing his servant. It is the centurion's faith that is important, rather than his nationality. This is echoed in Galatians 3:28 when Paul writes that faith in Jesus gives us all an equal opportunity to be part of the family of God. In Acts 2:1–13, the story of Pentecost, people from different nations find that they can all understand the message that the good news of Jesus is for everyone.

In this session we think about the fact that the qualification for being a part of God's family is not the possession of a particular type of passport but a belief in Jesus and a willingness to make him the king of our hearts. We are encouraged to develop an interest in, rather than a suspicion of, things that are new, strange or different and to respect people of other countries and their culture.

Go!

Display the small tree or branches, decorated with the stable and shepherd tree decorations that remind us of homelessness and loneliness. (Mention the stockings that the children might have made for a lonely neighbour or relative.) Who else is the gift of Christmas for? Perhaps the icebreaker will give us a clue.

Icebreaker

You will need

Six photographs of famous places in different countries, cut from travel brochures or magazines and placed around the room

Chat about countries the children may have visited. What did they find interesting or unusual about them? Ask the children to form pairs. Allow them plenty of time to look at the pictures and try to identify the place or building and the country where it is situated. Encourage them to take a guess if they don't know the answer. Next, look at each picture together. What is the collective name for the people who live in each country?

Dramatised Bible story

Explain that today's Bible story is all about the wise men coming to visit the baby Jesus. Before you read the story together, ask the children to listen carefully in order to discover whether or not the wise men came to Bethlehem from another country, and what they did when they found Jesus. The storytelling can be divided among several children.

Narrator 1:   When Jesus was born in the village of Bethlehem in Judea, Herod was king.

Narrator 2:   During this time some wise men from the east came to Jerusalem and said…

Wise man 1: Where is the child born to be king of the Jews?

Wise man 2: We saw his star in the east…

Wise man 3: And have come to worship him.

Narrator 1:   When King Herod heard about this, he was worried, and so was everyone else in Jerusalem.

Narrator 2:   Herod brought together the chief priests and the teachers of the Law of Moses and asked them…

Herod: Where will the Messiah be born?

Narrator 1:   They told him…

Teacher 1:   He will be born in Bethlehem, just as the prophet wrote…

Teacher 2:   Bethlehem in the land of Judea, you are very important among the towns of Judea.

Teacher 3:   From your town will come a leader, who will be like a shepherd for my people Israel.

Narrator 1:   Herod secretly called in the wise men and asked them when they had first seen the star. He told them…

Reproduced with permission from *Seasonal Activities for Christmas Festivities* by Vicki Howie (BRF/Barnabas, 2012)
www.barnabasinchurches.org.uk

Herod: Go to Bethlehem and search carefully for the child. As soon as you find him, let me know. I want to go and worship him, too.

Narrator 2: The wise men listened to what the king said and then left. And the star they had seen in the east went on ahead of them until it stopped over the place where the child was.

Narrator 1: They were thrilled and excited to see the star.

Narrator 2: When the men went into the house and saw the child with Mary his mother, they knelt down and worshipped him.

Narrator 1: They took out their gifts of gold, frankincense and myrrh and gave them to him.

Narrator 2: Later they were warned in a dream not to return to Herod, and they went back home by another road.

Follow-up discussion

Confirm that the wise men came from another country but that we don't know for sure which one. We only know that they came from the east, perhaps from Persia, Babylonia or Arabia. (You might like to point out these places on a map.) They returned to their country when they had visited baby Jesus.

This story could be said to give us a clue that Jesus came for people of every nation. Talk about how the wise men bowed down and worshipped Jesus and gave him precious gifts.

Reproduced with permission from *Seasonal Activities for Christmas Festivities* by Vicki Howie (BRF/Barnabas, 2012)
www.barnabasinchurches.org.uk

The gift of Christmas nativity scene

You will need

A nativity stable; a set of nativity figures

Choose some children to add the three wise men to the scene with the holy family and the shepherds.

Drama games

Greetings, Your Majesty!

You will need

A chair; a blindfold; a paper crown

This game is for at least five players. One child is selected to be king or queen and sits on the 'throne', wearing the crown and the blindfold. The other players sit together silently. When you signal to a child, he or she stands up, walks to the middle and, in a disguised voice, says, 'Greetings, Your Majesty!' If the king or queen guesses who that person is, the player sits down again. If the king or queen gets the name wrong, then it is that player's turn to be king or queen. (You may like to allow two guesses.)

Follow-up discussion

Discuss the wise men's meeting with King Herod. Explain that he was disturbed by the rumours of the birth of a great new king because he was worried that he would lose his throne. The angel Gabriel told Mary that Jesus would be a great king and that his kingdom would never end. Talk about how this kingdom is not somewhere that you can find on a map, like the other countries that you have been discussing. This special kingdom exists wherever people truly believe and trust in Jesus and try to live lives that please him. That could happen anywhere in the world.

Passport to happiness

Ask the children to sit down all around the room. Explain that you want them to imagine they are going to travel to a famous place or building that they have always wanted to visit in another country, such as Disney World in Florida or the Eiffel Tower in France. Allow them a few moments to decide on a particular place, and give anyone who needs it some help with ideas. Now ask them to mime the following story, taking care not to bump into anyone else.

Imagine you are sitting on an aeroplane, flying to your chosen destination. Have a look around you. Here comes the flight attendant with a snack for you. What is it? You eat it up… Now put your head back for a snooze… The plane is coming in to land now, so sit up straight and make sure that your seatbelt is fastened. The plane has come to a standstill, so stand up and take your bag from the overhead locker… Make your way to the door… walk down the steps… and walk to the terminal building.

You now join a long queue at passport control. As the queue creeps forward, you find your passport… and now you show it to the officer at the desk. He nods and you pass on through. You walk out of the airport and hail a taxi... You get in and the driver speeds you to the place that you have always wanted to visit... At last, you are there! You pay the taxi driver... and get out of the car.

You walk towards your chosen place or building. What does it look like? How does it make you feel? You go a little closer. Look all around you and notice every detail... Is anyone else there? What are they doing? What is the weather like? How does it compare with your own country? Spend some time enjoying this place in whatever way you like...

It's nearly time to leave now. Take a photograph to remind yourself of your visit... Later, you climb back up the steps into the aeroplane and find your seat... Your plane takes off and, before long, you are landing back at home. You look out of the window and see your own country again. What does it feel like to be back home again?

Follow-up discussion

Chat together about where the different children went on their imaginary journeys. What did they see? What did they do there? Did they have to show their passport to get into the country they visited? Do we need a passport to get into God's kingdom? Explain that God's special kingdom is not somewhere that we can visit in the same way as we visit another country, but something we can experience when we decide to make Jesus the king of our lives and try to follow in his footsteps.

Talk about how Jesus wants us to show respect towards and be ready to help people, wherever they come from, as he did. You may like to give an example, such as the story of Jesus healing the centurion's servant (Luke 7:1–10).

Fun food stations

Chat about favourite foods from other countries and set up some food stations on tabletops for everyone to enjoy. (NB: be aware of food allergies.)

Kebab station

You will need

Wooden skewers and a selection of colourful foods to thread on to them, such as stuffed olives, cubes of mozzarella cheese, cubes of green pepper, baby sweetcorn, salami, pieces of Frankfurter sausage and so on

Invite everyone to make a kebab with food of their choice. Encourage them to try something new.

Chopstick station

You will need

Chopsticks; small bowls; dried peas

Show how to hold the chopsticks in one hand. How many peas can the children pick up and move from one bowl to the other?

Bread station

You will need

French sticks; bagels; ciabatta rolls; English muffins; mini-pitta bread

Invite everyone to name the different types of bread. Which countries do they come from? Invite the children to sample bread of their choosing.

Getting to know you...

If your church supports a charity working in another country, you might like to ask a member of the congregation involved to come and talk for a few minutes about the work being done.

Individual craft

You will need

Traditional luggage labels or gift tags (one per child); gold thread or ribbon; gold paper cut into crown shapes; plain paper cut into heart shapes; patterned paper cut into cloak shapes; cotton wool; gold-wrapped sweets; sequins; glitter; crayons or felt-tipped pens; scissors; glue; sticky tape

Show the children a wise man tree decoration that you have made earlier (see example below) and hang it on the branches or tree to symbolise the idea that the good news of Christmas is offered to people of every nation.

To make the decoration, tie a loop of gold thread or ribbon through the hole in the label for hanging. Draw features on the heart shape for the face and glue it to the label, leaving room to glue the crown above it. Glue the patterned cloak shape over the lower part of the label. Glue tufts of cotton wool around the face for a beard. Decorate the cloak with sequins and glitter. Finally, tape the sweet to the centre of the cloak to look as if the wise man is holding a precious gift.

Prayer

Talk about the different things that we find in other countries, such as different foods, clothing, languages and so on. Chat about why this makes it so interesting to visit other countries or meet people from another country. What things might people be able to understand and appreciate wherever they come from in the world? Talk about things such as music and dance, the natural world, sport, and emotions such as love.

Dear God, thank you that you guided the wise men in a far country to find the baby Jesus. Please help us to appreciate our world, with all its interesting and different countries. Please make us ready to respect all people and to understand that we are all members of one big human family. Amen

Party bag

Using the internet, print out some small flags from different countries and give the children a selection to take home as a reminder of today's session. The flags could be used to decorate notebooks, stuck on to thin card to make bookmarks, attached to cocktail sticks to decorate sandwiches over Christmas or simply pinned to a bedroom noticeboard. Ask everyone to tell you next week how they used the flags.

★

The flight into Egypt

Theme
Refugees

Bible story
Matthew 2:13–23

Ready, steady...

A refugee is someone who has been forced to flee his or her country because of persecution, war or violence. In this session, the donkey, which may have been ridden by Mary on the journey to Egypt, is used as a symbol of those fleeing their homeland.

Refugees, including children, often need to leave their homes very quickly, although sometimes one family member may stay behind to look after farm animals. There may be no time to pack any possessions. The refugees may embark upon a long, uncomfortable and hazardous journey to another country. Having reached it, they may then live for a long time in a refugee camp. Here, a family may have to live in one room and eat just one meal a day, and there may be just one teacher for all the children.

Refugee children speak of being homesick, of missing a favourite place to play, their friends and their schools. They may suffer from teasing. Such children hope to be joined by the relative they left behind, to live in a better place with good teachers and to grow up to have good jobs. Most of all, they long to be accepted and to feel welcome and at home in a strange land.

Take time to look at the websites of some charities or agencies working with refugees. The UN Refugee Agency has a Teacher's Corner that includes videos of interviews with children. (Visit www.unhcr.org.uk.) The session concludes with the idea of God as a refuge for us all.

Go!

Display the small tree or branches decorated with the stable, shepherd and wise man tree decorations, which remind us of homelessness, loneliness and people from every nation. (Talk about how the children might have used the small flags from last week's party bag.) Who else did Jesus come to befriend? Perhaps the icebreaker game will give us a clue.

Icebreaker

You will need

A backpack containing six items that a child might take on a trip to help make them feel at home (such as a soft toy, a small photograph album, a blanket, a favourite DVD, a book and a game); paper and pencils

Chat about whether the children have ever spent the night away from home. Has anyone been away from home for longer? Did they feel homesick? Can they describe what it felt like? What do we miss about our homes or the place where we live when we go away? For example, we might miss a pet, a brother or sister, our own bed, our friends or a favourite toy or pastime.

Invite the children to make a list or draw several things that they would pack to stop themselves from feeling homesick if they were going away from home for a long trip. If anyone is stuck for ideas, let them have a look in the backpack. After a few minutes, chat about the items they would pack. Ask everyone to shout out 'snap' if they have packed the same sort of object that someone else mentions.

Next, explain that, in some countries, children sometimes have to leave their homes very quickly because their lives are in danger. This might be because a war is getting very close to their home or because there is a famine in their land. They may have to leave so quickly that there is no time to take anything with them except for the clothes they are wearing. They have to flee with their family to a place of safety that might be far from home and in another country. They might even have to leave their father behind, perhaps to look after a farm. Such people are known as refugees. Talk about pictures of refugees fleeing from their country that the children might have seen on television.

Dramatised Bible story

Our Bible story today is about three refugees. Ask everyone to listen carefully to find out who they were and what danger they were fleeing from. Explain that the story takes place soon after the wise men had offered their precious gifts to Jesus and had been warned to go back to their country by a different road. The storytelling can be divided among several children.

Narrator 1:   After the wise men had gone, an angel from the Lord appeared to Joseph in a dream and said…

Angel: Get up! Hurry and take the child and his mother to Egypt! Stay there until I tell you to return, because Herod is looking for the child and wants to kill him.

Reproduced with permission from *Seasonal Activities for Christmas Festivities* by Vicki Howie (BRF/Barnabas, 2012)
www.barnabasinchurches.org.uk
159

Narrator 2:   That night, Joseph got up and took his wife and the child to Egypt, where they stayed until Herod died.

Narrator 3:   When Herod found out that the wise men from the east had tricked him, he was very angry. He gave orders for his men to kill all the boys who lived in or near Bethlehem and were two years old and younger.

Narrator 4:   After King Herod died, an angel from the Lord appeared in a dream to Joseph while he was still in Egypt. The angel said...

Angel: Get up and take the child and his mother back to Israel. The people who wanted to kill him are now dead.

Narrator 5:   Joseph got up and left with them for Israel. But when he heard that Herod's son Archelaus was now ruler of Judea, he was afraid to go there.

Narrator 6:   Then, in a dream, he was told to go to Galilee, and they went to live there in the town of Nazareth.

Follow-up discussion

Talk about Joseph, Mary and baby Jesus fleeing to Egypt, Mary probably riding on a donkey and carrying Jesus in her arms. They were escaping from King Herod's soldiers, who had orders to kill baby Jesus. Herod was terrified that the new baby king would take his place on the throne.

Reproduced with permission from *Seasonal Activities for Christmas Festivities* by Vicki Howie (BRF/Barnabas, 2012)
www.barnabasinchurches.org.uk

The gift of Christmas nativity scene

You will need

A nativity stable; a set of nativity figures

Invite some children to add a donkey and any other animals to the scene, which should already include the holy family, the shepherds and the wise men.

Drama games

Marathon run

Introduce the idea of running a race, such as a marathon. Ask the children to find a space. Explain that everyone needs to run on the spot throughout this short game. Ask the children to start off at a lively pace, then slow down a bit and pretend to drink from a water bottle as they keep running. Ask them to imagine they are way out in front of the other runners; they wave to the crowds as they run at a comfortable pace. Everyone is getting tired now, so slow right down. Hurray! The finish line is in sight. The TV cameras are filming, so put on an extra spurt... and now run with both arms in the air to cross the finish line. Gradually come to a stop... shake out those arms and legs... then sit down and hug your knees.

Follow-up discussion

Ask the children to close their eyes and imagine what it would be like to be forced to run away from home because of danger nearby—running not because they want to but because they have to. Perhaps war is getting too close for comfort and bombs are dropping nearby; the sound of gunfire is getting louder. Perhaps there is no time to collect any favourite possessions; they must run with just the clothes that they happen to be wearing, as fast as they can in the hot sun. There's no knowing when (or if) they will get a drink; when (or if) they will see their friends again or the familiar places where they used to play. There may be hazards along the way. It might be very cold at night. The road might be very rough and pot-holed. They are running not towards the finish line but to the border with a safe country.

This country will be a safe place, a refuge. But they will have to start life all over again here, as a stranger in a country where they do not understand the language; perhaps they won't even recognise the alphabet. At least it will be safe, though. Ask everyone to open their eyes. They are all in the safety of the room. Talk about what it might feel like to be a refugee.

Refugee camp

You will need

Various objects with which the children can use their imagination to devise a game, such as wastepaper baskets, paper, string, chalk, pingpong ball, pencil, old mat and so on; paper; pens; a child's English/foreign language dictionary; some simple first aid equipment

Split the children into three groups and have the groups try out each of the following activities in rotation.

- In a refugee camp, children may have to make their own entertainment with whatever is available. Ask one of the groups to devise a simple game with a few rules and to try it out.

- Refugees often have to learn the language of the country in which they are now living. The younger you are, the easier it is to learn another language. For this reason, children often end up interpreting for their mothers when they take a brother or sister to the doctor. Ask the next group to look up three words in another language in the dictionary. They could write the words down and perhaps draw a picture to help them remember what each word means. They might spend some time learning these words and ask you to test them when they feel ready.
- Refugees might need medical help after their long journey. Depending on the skills of your helpers, show the children how to bandage a hand correctly or to make a sling, and let everyone have a go at doing it.

After a while, the teams swap over.

Craft activities

You will need

Traditional luggage labels or gift tags (one per child); string; card cut in the shape of donkey's ears (one pair per child); teabags; fake fur or cotton wool; felt-tipped pens; glue; scissors; orange sweets or long wrapped toffees

Show the children a donkey tree decoration that you have made earlier (see example below) and hang it on the tree or branches to symbolise the fact that the gift of Christmas is offered to all people, including refugees.

To make the decoration, tie a piece of string through the punched hole in the tag for hanging. Snip off the bottom corners of the tag (the end opposite the punched hole) to make a curved shape for the donkey's mouth. Draw two eyes about halfway up the tag and glue string across the face, above and below the eyes, for the head reins. Draw two black nostrils.

Cover the face (except for the nostril area) with glue and sprinkle with tea from a teabag. Glue or tape on the ears and glue a tuft of fake fur or cotton wool between the ears for the mane. Finally, tape the sweet to the back of the tag, so that it sticks out near the mouth and looks as if the donkey is eating a carrot.

Prayer

Chat together about feelings that people who are refugees might experience, either when they are fleeing from a dangerous situation or when they are living in another country—for example, frightened, homesick, sad, confused or bewildered, or like a stranger. Talk about what refugees might like to feel—for example, safe again, accepted and welcomed, at home even though they are far from home, hopeful that they might be able to go home again one day.

Dear God, thank you for watching over Mary, Joseph and baby Jesus when they fled to Egypt, and for bringing them safely back home to Nazareth. Help us to imagine what it must be like to be a refugee and to feel like a stranger in a faraway country. Please help all those who work with people who are refugees to make them feel welcome and at home. Amen

Party bag

Explain that we all feel anxious at times about things that we have to do. Perhaps we are joining a new school, moving house, spending Christmas at a different house or struggling with some difficult subjects at school. Remind everyone that God understands how we feel. He wants us to talk to him about these things. We can rely on him to give us the courage we need to face each situation. In this way, God can be a place of safety or refuge to us.

Give the children a strip of card, wider at the top than at the bottom, and cut a castellation shape along the top like the top of a castle tower. Near the top, write:

'God is… always ready to help in times of trouble.' (Psalm 46:1)

At home, the children could draw the outline of some large stones on the castle wall. If they are anxious about anything, they could write an appropriate word or draw an appropriate picture inside one of the outlines, to remind themselves to ask God for help with it and also to talk to a trusted adult. They might like to glue a photograph of themselves at the top of the tower. Encourage everyone to use the card as a bookmark and to memorise the verse.

The presentation in the temple

> **Theme**
> Each one of us
>
> **Bible story**
> Luke 2:21–40

Ready, steady...

Children had little status in Jewish society, but Jesus turned this idea on its head. In Matthew 11:25–30, Jesus praises God for the gift of the gospel to ordinary people who are humble and trusting. Again, in Mark 10:13–16, Jesus blesses little children and points out that the trustfulness displayed by a child is the right model for our relationship with God.

Jesus was born and died for each one of us; he is our personal Saviour. Psalm 139:1–18 reminds us of the depth of knowledge that God has about each of us. It follows that he must know the exact needs of each of us, too.

Go!

Display the small Christmas tree or bare branches, hung with the stable, shepherd, wise man and donkey tree decorations, reminding us of homeless people, lonely people, people of every nation and refugees. (Mention the Bible verse that was written on the castle bookmarks.) Who else did Jesus come to befriend? The icebreaker game may give us a clue.

Icebreaker

You will need

Photographs of babies, toddlers, young children, teenagers and adults (from young adults up to senior citizens) cut from magazines or catalogues; a baby doll, unclothed

Mix up all the photos. Ask the children to spend some time quietly looking at the photos and then to arrange them so that they go from 'young' on the left to 'elderly' on the right. Encourage any discussion arising from the photos about the children's earliest memories of their baby brothers or sisters, their grandparents and so on. Point out that, whatever age we are now, we all started life as a tiny baby.

Next, bring out the baby doll and remind the children that Jesus was born as a baby, just like all of us. Emphasise the helplessness of a baby compared with children of other ages, and chat together about what a baby needs in order to flourish, such as milk and then baby food for growth; clothing for warmth; regular bathing to keep clean and healthy; lots of sleep in a safe place; lots of love (which could include being held, cuddled, rocked, sung to and entertained). Talk about who provides all these necessary things. Point out that a baby depends totally on his or her parents.

Take the baby Jesus figure from the nativity scene and hold it in your hand. Talk about how God placed Jesus in a loving family, in which Mary and Joseph provided for all his infant needs.

Dramatised Bible story

Explain that today's Bible story involves a tiny baby and some elderly people. Before you read the story together, ask the children to listen carefully to find out who the youngest and oldest people in this story are, and who gives the baby a cuddle. The storytelling can be divided among several children:

Narrator 1:   Mary and Joseph named the baby Jesus, just as the angel Gabriel had told them to do.

Narrator 2:   They took Jesus to the temple in Jerusalem and presented him to the Lord.

Narrator 3:   This was one of the laws that God had given to Moses many years earlier.

Narrator 4:   They loved God and wanted to obey his laws, so they also took two young birds, either doves or pigeons, to offer to God.

Narrator 5:   Now there was an elderly man living in Jerusalem at that time, called Simeon. God had promised Simeon that he would not die before he had seen the Saviour with his own eyes.

Narrator 6:   On the day when Joseph and Mary took their baby to the temple, the Holy Spirit told Simeon to go to the temple, too.

Narrator 7:   When Joseph and Mary brought Jesus in, Simeon took him in his arms and praised God. He said…

Simeon: Now, Lord, your promise has come true. I have seen the Saviour! Now I can die in peace.

Narrator 1:   Joseph and Mary were amazed at all the things that Simeon said about Jesus and what he would do when he grew up.

Reproduced with permission from *Seasonal Activities for Christmas Festivities* by Vicki Howie (BRF/Barnabas, 2012)
www.barnabasinchurches.org.uk

Narrator 2: There was also an elderly woman, called Anna, at the temple that day.

Narrator 3: God sometimes told Anna about things that would happen in the future. She was 84 years old.

Narrator 4: Anna worshipped in the temple night and day, fasting and praying. She came up to Simeon just as he was holding baby Jesus and talking to Joseph and Mary.

Narrator 5: Gazing at Jesus, she began to give thanks to God for letting her see his Son. Later, she told all her friends that she had seen the special baby who was going to grow up to be everyone's friend.

Narrator 6: When Joseph and Mary had done everything the law required, they returned to Galilee to their home town of Nazareth.

Narrator 7: As Jesus grew, he became strong and wise, and God blessed him.

Follow-up discussion

Jesus was a baby (probably about six weeks old) at the beginning of the story. We don't know how old Simeon was, but Anna was 84 years old. Chat together about how Simeon took Jesus in his arms. God had made sure that Simeon was in the right place at the right time. Talk about how Simeon and Anna had a close relationship with God, so perhaps they could sense God telling them that this was the baby they had been waiting to see for so long. Talk about how they were full of thanks and joy and how Anna told others about her exciting meeting in the temple. They received the Christmas gift with open arms.

Reproduced with permission from *Seasonal Activities for Christmas Festivities* by Vicki Howie (BRF/Barnabas, 2012)
www.barnabasinchurches.org.uk

The gift of Christmas nativity scene

> ### You will need
>
> A nativity stable; a set of nativity figures

Choose someone to replace the baby Jesus in the manger.

Drama games

Lucky dip!

> ### You will need
>
> A selection of biblical names (enough for one per child) written on pieces of paper, which are folded and placed in a container; a baby name book

Explain that you are going to play a name game, as the story today involved Jesus being given his name. Invite everyone to select a piece of paper from the container but not to unfold it yet.

Ask the children to spread out around the room, holding their folded papers. Next, ask everyone to walk and count eight steps. Now they shake hands and introduce themselves to someone nearby. As they do so, they should unfold the paper and read out the name. For example, they say, 'Hello, I'm... (unfold the paper) Moses!' or 'Hello, I'm... King Solomon!'

Allow the game to continue in this manner, using the names, for a while. Then explain that the children must swap names after they have met each new person. For example, one says, 'Hello, my name is Noah!' The other says, 'Hello, my name is Simeon.' They then swap pieces of paper, so that Noah becomes Simeon and vice versa. They must introduce themselves to the next person they meet, using their new name.

The game continues, swapping names each time. Finally, ask everyone to see if they can continue without the pieces of paper. This will test their concentration, listening and memory skills.

Follow-up discussion

Explain that names and their meanings were very important in biblical times. Chat about what the children's own names mean, using a baby name book for reference if necessary. Talk about what Jesus' name means ('God saves'). Jesus shows us how to lead lives that please God and to enjoy being part of his family. Jesus is sometimes called 'Immanuel' in the Bible (meaning 'God with us'), since, in Jesus, God came into the world as a tiny baby. Remind the children that Jesus knows each of us by name. He came for each and every one of us, young and old.

Jesus welcomes children

> ### You will need
>
> The baby doll from the icebreaker activity; a baby's blanket

Everyone shows how welcome children are in different places by calling out the word 'welcome'. The louder they speak, the more welcome they think children are in that place. Places could include a quiet library, playground, restaurant, school, church, hotel and so on. Then ask the group to act out the story below as you read it aloud.

Before you start, choose children to be Jesus (seated on a chair);

a crowd listening to Jesus (seated on the floor around him); some disciples (standing behind the crowd); some children with their mother holding the baby doll wrapped in a baby's blanket (at the far end of the room).

It was a very hot day. Jesus sat under a shady tree in the market square, telling a wonderful story about God to all the people crowded around him. He was telling them how much God loved them all. As he spoke, he smiled and looked each one of them in the eyes so that everyone felt as if the story was just for them. Jesus moved his hands about to show that God's kingdom would start very small… but would grow and grow until it was enormous.

The disciples stood at the back of the crowd, arms folded, watching Jesus and sometimes looking round to make sure that no one came to disturb him. A mother came walking into the square, holding her baby. Her other children followed her. They stopped when they saw the crowd.

'Who is that telling a story?' the children asked their mother.

Their mother looked surprised. 'Why! It's Jesus!' she said. 'Let's go and listen to what he is saying. I'm sure he will bless the baby.'

But as the family came up to join the crowd, the disciples looked round and waved them away.

'Quiet! Don't disturb Jesus!' they said. 'Can't you see that he's busy?'

The family began to turn away, but then something amazing happened. Jesus stood up and spoke to his disciples. The crowd looked around at them.

'Let the little children come to me,' he said. 'Don't try to stop them!'

So the crowd parted and, shyly, the mother and her children went right up to Jesus. Jesus held out his arms to welcome them. Then he put his hands on the children's heads to bless them.

At last, he took the baby in his arms. 'People who are like these little children belong to the kingdom of God,' he said. 'I promise you that you cannot get into God's kingdom unless you accept it the way a child does.'

Follow-up discussion

Chat together about the way Jesus welcomes children and how important they are to him. Ask, 'How welcome are children in God's kingdom?' and encourage everyone to raise the roof as they reply, 'Very welcome!' Talk about how God wants us to rely on him for all we need, in the same way that a baby relies on its parents.

Craft activities

You will need

Traditional luggage labels or gift tags (one per child); blue crayons; circles of white paper; strips of raffia; silver or coloured star stickers; round sweets wrapped in gold paper; crayons; glue

Show the children a baby Jesus tree decoration that you have made earlier (see example below). Hang it on your tree or bare branches to show that Jesus was born as a baby and came for each and every one of us.

To make the decoration, tie a strip of raffia on the tag for hanging. Colour the tag blue. Draw features on the paper circle to make the baby's face and glue it to the middle of the tag. Glue on strips of raffia in a V shape below the face to make it seem as if Jesus is looking out of a manger full of straw. Stick some stars in the sky and glue the sweet above the baby's head as a halo.

Prayer

Invite everyone to gather around the tree or branches with all five decorations attached. Jesus is God's Christmas gift to everyone, including homeless people, lonely people, those from every nation, refugees and ourselves, young and old.

Dear God, Christmas is nearly here and we want to thank you for sending us the gift of your Son to be our friend and to show us how to live. As we grow up, help us to make sure we also grow closer to you, so that we get to know you better and begin to understand what you want us to do in our lives. Help us to remember that Jesus knows each of us by name and wants to be our friend. Just as Simeon held out his arms to receive Jesus as a baby, help us to welcome Jesus into our homes and lives this Christmas. Amen

Party bag

Give the children a personal Christmas card or a small gift. Make sure that their name is on it to emphasise the personal aspect. Encourage everyone to make personal cards or gifts for members of their families during the Christmas holidays.

✦

The gift of Christmas

Display the small tree or bare branches in a prominent position in readiness for hanging the five tree decorations. As well as holding up the various tree decorations where shown, you might like to project a picture of a blank gift tag, a stable, a shepherd, a wise man, a donkey and baby Jesus on a screen.

Narrator 1: At the first Christmas, God sent a wonderful present to the earth.

All: Good news!

Narrator 2: The present was his own Son, Jesus, bringing kindness and friendship.

Narrator 3: But who was this present for? (*Hold up a blank gift tag*)

Narrator 4: We have decorated five gift tags to symbolise the different people God cares about.

Narrator 1: First of all, we read about the census ordered by Emperor Augustus.

Narrator 2: Everyone had to go to his home town to be listed. So Joseph and Mary travelled to Bethlehem, because that was where Joseph's family came from.

Narrator 3: While they were there, the time came for Mary's baby to be born, but Bethlehem was packed and there was no room for them to stay at the inn. Mary and Joseph had nowhere to stay.

Reproduced with permission from *Seasonal Activities for Christmas Festivities* by Vicki Howie (BRF/Barnabas, 2012)
www.barnabasinchurches.org.uk

Narrator 4:   Someone took pity on them and the Son of God was born in a borrowed stable and laid in a borrowed manger.

Narrator 1:   We thought about what it must be like to be homeless…

Child 1:   Nowhere to shelter.

Child 2:   Nothing to eat.

Child 3:   Nowhere to wash.

Child 4:   Nowhere to call your own.

Narrator 2:   So we made a stable tree decoration (*hold it up*) to remind us to pray for homeless people this Christmas.

Hang the decoration on the tree. Pause.

Narrator 3:   Next, we read about some people who lived a very lonely life.

All: The shepherds!

Narrator 4:   The shepherds were living out in the fields on the fringes of the town, keeping watch over their flocks.

Narrator 1:   Suddenly, an angel appeared to them and said…

Angel: Don't be afraid! I have good news for you, which will make everyone happy. This very day in King David's town a Saviour was born for you. He is Christ the Lord. You will know who he is, because you will find him dressed in baby clothes and lying on a bed of hay.

Narrator 2:   The shepherds hurried into Bethlehem to find Jesus.

Reproduced with permission from *Seasonal Activities for Christmas Festivities* by Vicki Howie (BRF/Barnabas, 2012)
www.barnabasinchurches.org.uk

Narrator 3: We thought about people who lead lonely lives
or sometimes feel left out…
Child 1: Elderly people.
Child 2: People with disabilities.
Child 3: People who care for others.
Narrator 4: We made a shepherd tree decoration (*hold it up*)
to remind us that the good news of Christmas is
for everyone.

Hang the decoration on the tree. Pause.

Narrator 1: Next, we read about the wise men who followed
a star to find baby Jesus.
Narrator 2: We found out that they journeyed to Bethlehem
from a distant country.
Narrator 3: We don't know which country it was, but it
may have been Persia, Babylonia or Arabia.
Narrator 4: When the wise men found Jesus, they bowed
down to worship him because they knew he
was God's chosen king.
Narrator 1: We discovered that Jesus' kingdom is not a
place you can find on a map. It exists wherever
people believe and trust in him. That could be
anywhere in the world.
Narrator 2: We made a wise man tree decoration (*hold it up*)
to remind us that the good news of Christmas is
offered to people of every nation.

Hang the decoration on the tree. Pause.

Narrator 4: Next, we read about the flight into Egypt.

Reproduced with permission from *Seasonal Activities for Christmas Festivities* by Vicki Howie (BRF/Barnabas, 2012)
www.barnabasinchurches.org.uk

Narrator 1:   When the wise men had left for their own country, baby Jesus was suddenly in great danger. Jealous King Herod planned to find him and kill him.

Narrator 2:   So God told Joseph to take his family to Egypt, where they would be safe. Mary probably rode on their donkey, carrying the baby in her arms.

Narrator 3:   They were refugees, since they were running for their lives to a place of safety.

Narrator 4:   We thought about how it must feel to be a refugee today, running away from everything that you know and love…

Child 1:   Your home.

Child 2:   Your friends.

Child 3:   People who speak your own language.

Narrator 1:   We made a donkey tree decoration (*hold it up*) to remind us to pray for people who are refugees this Christmas.

Hang the decoration on the tree. Pause.

Narrator 2:   Finally, we read about Mary and Joseph naming baby Jesus and presenting him at the temple.

Narrator 3:   There, an elderly man named Simeon took the baby into his arms with great joy. Somehow he knew that this was God's promised Saviour.

Narrator 4:   Jesus was born as a baby, just like us

Narrator 1:   He came to be our friend and Saviour.

Narrator 2:   We made a baby Jesus tree decoration (*hold it up*) to show that the good news of Christmas is for each one of us, young and old.

Hang the decoration on the tree. Pause.

Leader: Dear God, Christmas is here! Thank you for sending us the wonderful gift of your Son. Help us to remember that you know each of us by name and that you want to be our friend. Help us to trust you for all that we need, in the same way that a baby trusts in its parents. Just as Simeon held out his arms to receive Jesus, so may we welcome Jesus into our homes and lives this Christmas by serving others and living lives that would gladden his heart. Amen

Reproduced with permission from *Seasonal Activities for Christmas Festivities* by Vicki Howie (BRF/Barnabas, 2012)
www.barnabasinchurches.org.uk

Easy Ways to Christmas Plays Volume 2

Three easy-to-perform plays for 3–7s

The festive season brings with it the opportunity to put on a simple nativity play with 3–7s. Following the success of Vicki Howie's ever-popular *Easy Ways to Christmas Plays*, this second book contains three brand new plays, each with a storyline that is woven around the Christmas story. A five-week countdown begins with the play written as a delightful story for you to read to the children, continues with simple drama games that take the place of long rehearsals, and ends with an easy-to-do performance of the play. The emphasis is on having fun while learning about many aspects of Christmas—an enjoyable nativity play being a welcome byproduct!

Choose from three exciting themes:

- **The Advent calendar puzzle:** An easy play that can be produced with a very small number of children if necessary. Prompted by the pictures behind the 24 doors, the children will discover which things are truly part of the Christmas story.
- **What can I give him?** Based on the tradition of Posada, this simple play will help children to understand that the best Christmas present we can give Jesus is to be kind to others.
- **Silent night:** A delightful play about the origins of this famous carol and why it was first performed with a guitar accompaniment.

ISBN 978 1 84101 585 9   £11.99

Available from your local Christian bookshop or direct from BRF: please visit www.brfonline.org.uk.

Silent Night

Illustrated by Krisztina Kállai Nagy

A delightful gift book version of the story of 'Silent night', featured in Vicki Howie's *Easy Ways to Christmas Plays Volume 2*.

'Long ago, inside a dusty mousehole, hidden in the church of St Nicholas, which stood in the village of Oberndorf, beside a river that rushed helter-skelter through a land of music, mountains and snow called Austria, there lived a large family of mice.'

This is the story of the mice that inspired the writing and singing of the Christmas carol, 'Silent night', beautifully illustrated by Hungarian-born Krisztina Kállai Nagy.

ISBN 978 1 84101 705 1   £7.99
Available from your local Christian bookshop or direct from BRF: please visit www.brfonline.org.uk.

Enjoyed

this book?

Write a review—we'd love to hear what you think.
Email: reviews@brf.org.uk

Keep up to date—receive details of our new books as they happen.
Sign up for email news and select your interest groups at:
www.brfonline.org.uk/findoutmore/

Follow us on Twitter @brfonline

By post—to receive new title information by post (UK only), complete
the form below and post to: BRF Mailing Lists, 15 The Chambers, Vineyard,
Abingdon, Oxfordshire, OX14 3FE

Your Details
Name _____
Address_____
_____
Town/City _____ Post Code _____
Email_____

Your Interest Groups (*Please tick as appropriate)	
☐ Advent/Lent	☐ Messy Church
☐ Bible Reading & Study	☐ Pastoral
☐ Children's Books	☐ Prayer & Spirituality
☐ Discipleship	☐ Resources for Children's Church
☐ Leadership	☐ Resources for Schools

Support your local bookshop
Ask about their new title information schemes.